KU-548-314

An Introduction to Marital Problems

Dr Jack Dominian is Senior Consultant Psychiatrist at the Central Middlesex Hospital. In 1971 he established the Marriage Research Centre, of which he is director. His books include *Depression, Marital Breakdown, Christian Marriage, Cycles of Affirmation, Proposals for a New Sexual Ethic, From Cosmos to Love* (with A. R. Peacocke), *Marital Pathology* and *Marriage, Faith and Love.*

An Introduction to Marital Problems

Dr J. Dominian, F.R.C.P.Ed., F.R.C.Psych., D.Sc (Hon)

Director of the Marriage Research Centre

NEWARK COMMUNITY
MENTAL HEALTH TEAM
SOCIAL SERVICES
RECEIVED
MAR 1989

Collins
FOUNT PAPERBACKS

First published by Fount Paperbacks, London in 1986
Copyright © Jack Dominian 1986

Made and printed in Great Britain by
William Collins Sons & Co. Ltd, Glasgow

Conditions of sale
This book is sold subject to the condition
that it shall not, by way of trade or otherwise,
be lent, re-sold, hired out or otherwise circulated
without the publisher's prior consent in any form of
binding or cover other than that in which it is
published and without a similar condition
including this condition being imposed
on the subsequent purchaser

NEWARK COMMUNITY
MENTAL HEALTH TEAM
SOCIAL SERVICES
RECEIVED
MAR 1988

Contents

Introduction

There has always been marital breakdown in society, and divorce has been considered a private affair involving the members of the family only. As the causes of marital breakdown are beginning to be understood, there is an increasing desire to seek help. This help involves large numbers of people who often go to their doctors, community nurses and health visitors, social workers and various experts.

In fact the caring professions have to bear the brunt of the consequences of marital conflict and breakdown. These consequences are often physical and mental ill-health, which require treatment in their own right, whilst the background marital problems need to be examined, understood and assisted.

In general the caring professions have not been trained for this work, and they are often faced with intricate marital problems which are hard to grasp and to assist. Given that each year over half a million people are involved in divorce, the number of the population who need help is extensive.

At present there is no book which introduces marital problems to the caring professions, those which exist being written for people who already have a background in dynamic psychology.

This textbook aims to be such an introduction, bringing together the essentials from different disciplines and emphasizing the practical, clinical implications of the work. It has been kept deliberately short so that it can be easily read. The extensive references can be used by those interested for further development of their knowledge.

The book is not meant to be the final word on the subject, which is continually expanding, nor does it aim to transform members of the caring professions into accomplished marriage counsellors. Further training is needed for that. Its aim, as the title suggests, is to be an introduction which leaves the reader better informed, able to cope with emergencies, and equipped to make use of courses on the subject of marital pathology. It is also meant to give an insight into the topic to non-clinicians interested in it.

The author is entirely responsible for the contents, but has been greatly assisted by the staff of the Marriage Research Centre at the Central Middlesex Hospital and by Mr Robert Chester who kindly read the book.

J. Dominian
Director
Marriage Research Centre
Central Middlesex Hospital
July 1985

Section 1

1. Marriage and Divorce

Marriage

The majority of women and men in Great Britain marry. Of the cohorts of women born between 1930 and 1950, about 90 per cent had married by the age of 30, and about 90 per cent of men born between 1930 and 1946 had married or will have married by the age of 40 (OPCS, *Marriage and Divorce Statistics*, 1980). Hidden within this overall rate there are fluctuations, mainly due to the ages at which people marry. Thus throughout the 1950s there was an upward trend in marriage rates, particularly for those under the age of 25. In the 1960s the teenage marriage rate continued to increase, but since the 1970s there has been a decline in marriage rates at ages under 30, particularly for those who are under 25. In particular the teenage rate has fallen by 55 per cent between 1971 and 1981. The marriage rate for 20- to 24-year-old women, the commonest age at which women marry, has fallen by 41 per cent over the same period. The behaviour of recent generations indicates that there is a decreased propensity to marry at early ages, and the trend appears to be continuing at a rapid pace with, as yet, little sign of slowing down (Kiernan, 1983).

Cohabitation

The decline in marriage rates is a feature which coincides with a rise in cohabitation. The most detailed study of cohabitation comes from the General Household Survey 1979 (Brown & Kiernan, 1981). First-time brides who married bachelors in the early 1970s showed an incidence of 7 per cent of premarital cohabitation. This figure rises to 19 per cent for brides who married in the period 1977–79. There is no evidence, however, that cohabitation has supplanted marriage, although it may postpone it. For example, after the high rate of marriage between 1961 and 1971, there was a drop of first marriages for both partners in 1976, a figure that has since remained relatively steady (Table 1).

Table 1

	Marriages in thousands for the United Kingdom					
	1961	1971	1976	1980	1981	1982
First marriages for both partners	340	369	282	279	263	255

Divorce

There are three main factors related to recent trends in marriage, namely the decrease in marriages of young people, particularly teenagers; an increase in cohabitation; and thirdly an increase in the rate of divorce. It is this feature which is the main concern of this book, and the demographical details will be considered in detail.

The most remarkable phenomenon of the 1970s has been the increase in divorce (Table 2).

Table 2

	Decrees Absolute Granted (thousands)						
	1961	1971	1976	1979	1980	1982	1983
England & Wales	25	74	127	139	148	147	147
Scotland	2	5	9	9	11	11	13
Northern Ireland	0.1	0.3	0.6	0.8	0.9	1.4	1.5

(Source: *Social Trends*, No. 15, HMSO, 1985)

The rise in divorce in the 1970s coincided with the Divorce Reform Act which came into force in England and Wales in 1971. The Act made irretrievable breakdown of marriage the sole ground for dissolution. It is arguable whether the Act facilitated divorce or whether the social trends in society made the Act inevitable. Either way it is currently calculated that on present figures approximately one in three of marriages are heading for dissolution (Haskey, 1982).

Divorce and Children

With the increase in divorce in the 1970s, the number of children involved in divorcing families has increased dramatically. The total number of children who experience divorce in their family in England and Wales is currently around 160,000 per year (*Social Trends*, No. 15). In a more detailed study it has been shown that, by the age of 16, one in five children will experience divorce in their families (Haskey, 1985). If one combines the number of adults and children involved in divorce annually, then a figure approaching half a million people is involved. Of course not all the children of divorced families will remain with their single parents: some will become part of reconstituted families as their parents remarry.

Single Parent Family

There are three sources of one-parent families, namely those that arise from separation/divorce, from death of the spouse and from the never-married. The single most important cause of single parents comes undoubtedly from the dissolution of marriage, with the child or children often going with the mother. Nearly 12 per cent of all families with dependent children were one-parent families in 1979–81, compared with 8 per cent in 1971–73. It is calculated that in 1979–81 there were 890,000 one-parent families, of which 87 per cent were headed by the mother.

Remarriage

A high proportion of those who divorce remarry. A sample of one thousand divorces granted in 1973 were followed for 4½ years (Leete & Anthony, 1979), and within this span of time, more than half had remarried, the proportion being higher for men. The younger the age at divorce, the higher is the chance of remarriage. Thus, whilst 55.5 per cent of all men in the sample remarried, those who had married for the first time under the age of 20 had a much higher proportion of remarriage, namely 69 per cent. This is also seen in women. The presence of children is no barrier to remarriage. Amongst the remarried, 90 per cent had civil weddings. What is the success of remarriage? Second marriages are in fact more vulnerable. The chance that the marriage of a divorced man would again end in divorce is one and a half times that of a single man who marries at the same age. Analogously, a divorced woman who remarries is approximately twice as likely to divorce as a single woman who marries at the same age (Haskey, 1983).

Specific Factors Associated with Divorce

So far the demographical details relating to marriage and divorce have been given. Next, the factors associated with marital breakdown are examined. The presence of these factors does not inevitably mean that marital breakdown will follow. It does mean that there is a statistical association between the two. Those who enter marriage in the presence of the adverse factors carry a statistical risk, and should be aware that they are more vulnerable than others. It also goes without saying that these are the men and women who need more support and care for their marriages.

Age at Marriage

Most studies have shown a close association between age at marriage and marital breakdown. This fact has been confirmed in the United Kingdom (Thornes & Collard, 1979) and in the United States of America (Glick & Norton, 1971). When the bride is under the age of 20 the chance of divorce is higher, and this is a risk that is increased still further if the groom is also under the age of 20. In this respect it is good to note the drop in teenage marriages referred to already.

Premarital Pregnancy

Couples who have conceived before marriage are more vulnerable to marital breakdown than those who have conceived after marriage. Similarly, those who conceive early after marriage run a greater risk than those who have their children at a later stage (Christensen, 1973; Thornes & Collard, 1979).

Youthful Marriage and Premarital Pregnancy

Whilst both youthful marriage and premarital pregnancy increase the risk of marital breakdown as individual factors, when they are combined the risk becomes higher still (Rowntree, 1964; Thornes & Collard, 1979).

Duration and Quality of Courtship

There is evidence that the duration and quality of courtship is a predictor of the future of marriage. Thus, short courtships, i.e. those without a sufficient period for the couples to get to know each other, are risky propositions. The same applies to marriages where there has been no engagement or honeymoon. In particular, the study of Thornes & Collard (1979) showed that, when there is persistent opposition to the pending marriage – particularly parental in origin – then the marriage is more vulnerable. Finally, the quality of the courtship is a suggestive indicator. When the courtship is stormy and punctuated by frequent break-ups, then the future outcome is more risky.

Social Class

In the United States more than one study has shown an inverse relationship between social class and marital stability (Bernard, 1966). In Britain the results indicate that there is a vulnerability associated with social class V and III n-m (Thornes & Collard, 1979). Thus, both in the United States and in Great Britain the lowest social class seems fragile. It is, of course, in the ranks of this social class that the youthful marriages and early pregnancies take place which are loading factors against marital stability. This is also the social class that is likely to have higher unemployment and poor housing, which will adversely affect the early stability of the marriage. In contrast, marriages in which the husband is highly educated appear to be more stable.

Religion

Marriages in which both parties are affiliated to a particular religion, particularly when the couple are churchgoers, are more stable (Thornes & Collard, 1979).

General Factors Associated with Divorce

The factors mentioned above have all been shown to be statistically related to the instability of marriage. These are clearly associated with marital breakdown, although no individual couple showing these features can be told categorically at their wedding that their marriage will not endure. If there is an element of uncertainty about the influence of these factors, there is an even greater speculation concerning the general factors underlying divorce. The fact is that, in the last twenty-five years, a wave of divorce has swept Western society which needs some explanation. The rate of breakdown appears to have stabilized now at this elevated level, which seems to be saying something fundamental about the nature of marriage and the expectations of couples. It is these more speculative elements that will now be considered.

Changing Nature of Marriage

Can any observation be made about the nature of marriage itself? Traditionally marriage has been considered to be an institution in which – at least since the post-industrial era – the spouses have had specific roles. Thus the husband has been considered to be the provider, the person who worked outside the home, the head of the family and its external ambassador. The wife has been seen to play the role of mother, housewife and the source of affection in the family. Given that the couple had children, remained faithful to each other and had a stable relationship, then they were considered to have a "good" marriage. This has been called the "instrumental" variety of marriage, and has been held as a "norm" for a long time.

Recently this variety of marriage has begun to change in many ways. Spouses are seeking a far more egalitarian relationship. Both spouses are now striving for equity in communication, discussion, decision-making and the general sharing of power. This sharing of power has been affected by the increase in the number of women working, who in turn are not so economically dependent on their spouses for survival.

The greater social access which the couples have to one another also has psychological repercussions. Their social closeness is reflected in a psychological intimacy, and this intimacy is vital in understanding contemporary marriage. There are two emotionally intimate relationships in life. The first is between the child and its parents, and the second is that between the spouses. The spouses are now so emotionally close to each other that they repeat many of the emotional interactions which they learned in their family of origin. This dynamic interaction between spouses today is much more realizable as husband and wife relate to each other more closely. **The various dynamic schools have based their understanding of the nature of marital difficulties through interpreting in the here and now relationship the psychological difficulties which the couple have brought to each other from their individual pasts.**

The greater intimacy which exists between couples today is not only reflected in their social and emotional lives but in their sexual expectations as well. This type of emerging marriage, which is shifting towards equity, intimacy and greater sexual satisfaction, is coming to be known as the "companionship" variety.

When we look at marriage today there is an admixture between the instrumental and companionship types, and each marriage has to be treated on the basis of what the couple expect from each other. Indeed, part of the overall marital difficulties is the problem that spouses may have different expectations, with men in general seeking the instrumental variety and women yearning for a more companionate form.

Women

The general emancipation of women has been documented in the increase in higher education, work and legal equality. In the field of marriage there is evidence that women are much more aware of marital problems (Thornes & Collard, 1979) and more articulate in declaring their presence (Brannen & Collard, 1982). There is also unequivocal evidence that they instigate the divorce process more often. The proportion of petitions filed by wives in England and Wales in 1983 was about seven out of ten, the same as in earlier years (*Social Trends*, No. 15). This tendency for women to seek petitions of divorce is explained away by solicitors on legal grounds, but the clinical evidence supports the alternative explanation that women are much more likely to protest against unsatisfactory marriages and are not prepared to put up with relationships that they would have endured in a previous generation.

Men, Women and Material Standards

Reference has been made to the fact that women are more prone to seek dissolution in an unsatisfactory marriage than they were in the past, and this is a reflection of higher material expectations. These expectations are not confined to women alone. In the last twenty-five years material standards in the West have risen. Currently unemployment is taking its toll, but overall the material quality of life has improved. When food, housing and work are available, there is a tendency to seek fulfilment at a deeper level of satisfaction. Thus, with material needs met, there is a yearning for fulfilment at the emotional and sexual level. The increase in sexual counselling both in the U.S.A. and Britain is one of the factors suggestive that couples want more out of their marriage than they did in the past.

People don't change overnight. It is worth speculating that one of the reasons for the increase in divorce has been the gap between rapidly rising expectations in the social, emotional and sexual quality of marriage, and the preparation and education to meet adequately these greater hopes.

Whatever the reason, the unprecedented rise in divorce in the last twenty-five years has steadied but is showing no visible sign of decline.

2. Dynamic and Other Factors Contributing to Marital Breakdown

In the previous chapter reference was made to the fact that the nature of marriage is slowly changing from an instrumental to a companionship variety. In the companionship variety the couple relive in their marriage emotional experiences reflecting the positive and negative feelings they had in their childhood. Hence dynamic psychologists pay enormous attention to the type of childhood the spouses had. Often the first intimate experience is repeated in the second one, between husband and wife. This is the object-relations theory in which the child learns, usually from mother but also from father, how to feel loved. When the early experiences are good, there is a high chance that the subsequent ones in the marriage will also be good but, when the childhood has been traumatic, then the intimacy of the marriage may resurrect the adverse feelings of childhood. These difficulties are not often present in the courtship or even in the early years of marriage, when the couple are in a state of being in love. The heightened and idealized awareness of each other eliminates any difficulties. But, as the couple move from the state of having fallen in love to loving, then slowly difficulties emerge. In order to understand these difficulties, the developmental aspects of the personality have now to be considered.

Dynamic Development of the Personality

A number of British and American psychologists have given us an outline of the feelings of the child in its early years. These experiences are often not actually remembered, but in the marital intimacy they are relived between the spouses. In what follows, the various contributions are described, from the first year of life onwards.

First Year of Life

The first year of life is critical for the formation of an affectionate bond between child and mother. According to traditional Freudian theory, this bond was formed because the child needed the food provided by the mother. Bowlby provides us with a different theory, namely attachment behaviour. Attachment behaviour is conceived as any form of behaviour that results in a person attaining or retaining proximity to some other differentiated and preferred individual, who is usually conceived as stronger and/or wiser. Whilst especially evident during early childhood, attachment behaviour is held to characterize human beings from cradle to grave.

The young baby forms an affectionate attachment, or falls in love, with its mother by holding and being held, watching and being watched, recognizing her voice and being responded to when it cries, and through smell. Through these physical parameters an affectionate bond is formed. When the child cries, the mother runs to its support; when it is frightened it seeks the proximity of mother or mother-substitute and, in this way, there is a closeness between the two which is interpreted as love. Whenever people fall in love they are attracted by the body visually, the voice, they want to touch each other and whisper attractive words. Thus Bowlby's theory illuminates the concept of falling in love which we learn in the first few weeks of life (Bowlby, 1979).

Another British psychoanalyst, Winnicott, added further details to the child's early experience. The baby has the capacity for emotional growth but it needs the mother's facilitating environment. This means that the mother provides food and love. For Winnicott, the child experiences love in terms of existing, breathing and being alive. Love means appetite and food, in other words, the need for satisfaction. As with Bowlby, for Winnicott love also means affectionate concern for the mother. This affectionate involvement means an integration on the part of the infant in which the mother is experienced both as an instinctual object and also as a source of affection. This relationship of instinct and affection will become crucial later on in marriage, in terms of sex and love. Finally, loving means the ability of the child to care for the mother as the mother cares for the infant, which is a preview of the adult reciprocal attitude of responsibility. The mother contributes to these experiences of love by holding and handling the child. Satisfactory holding is basic to care, faulty holding produces extreme distress to the infant, giving a basis for the sense of going to pieces, the sense of falling for ever, the feeling that external reality cannot be used for reassurance. Later on, in the intimacy of marriage, spouses will describe sensations in which they feel insecure in the presence of their spouse which, up to a point, are contributed by the type of physical handling they receive from their partner (Winnicott, 1965). For example, when they are held they do not feel safe in the arms of their spouse.

Still staying in the first year of life, the American psychoanalyst Erikson (1968) considers that this is the phase when the child acquires the sense of trust. Both Bowlby and

Winnicott hint at the child's development of the sense of trust through its relationship with mother, but Erikson makes trust the key experience of the first year of life. The amount of trust derived from the earliest infantile experience does not seem to depend on absolute quantities of food or demonstration of love, but rather on the quality of the maternal relationship. Mothers create a sense of trust in their children by combining sensitive care of the baby's individual needs and a firm sense of personal trustworthiness within the framework of their culture's life style. The sense of trust imbued by the mother grows gradually, and the physical trust is carried over into verbal trustworthiness. One of the essential ingredients of human love is our ability to trust another person, and the reciprocal trust of spouses is a vital component of their love for each other. When a husband or wife betrays this love by having an affair or telling lies, then the spouse may find it very difficult to establish trust anew.

All these writers are describing how the infant senses the somatic instinctual experiences of the first year as love. In more poetic language, Karen Horney (1969) writes of the child's need for unconditional love.

Second and Third Years of Life

In terms of Freud and his principal successor in Britain, Melanie Klein (1957, 1965), feelings of envy and jealousy arise in the first year of life. In the theoretical model pursued here, these are experiences of the second and third years of life. Envy is a dyad, a one-to-one relationship in which the child is aware of its smallness, powerlessness, helplessness compared to mother, accompanied by intense feelings of anger and competition. Feelings of envy exist in adult relationships between spouses, and cause a sense of competition and irritation. Jealousy is basically a triangular situation which can often arise at the advent of a sister or brother during these years, or later on. Adults sometimes carry marked memories of favoured siblings who were preferred by their parents. These feelings persist in adult life, with the man or woman experiencing a deep sense of inferiority compared to others who are considered more attractive or intelligent, despite evidence to the contrary.

The importance of the second and third years is, however, much greater than the origins of envy and jealousy. If we consider the growth of the person as a gradual separation between itself and its parents, then during these two years the child learns to crawl, stand up, walk, run, feed and dress itself, and to control defecation. This is Freud's anal stage. For Erikson, all these activities are part of what he calls the phase of autonomy. It is during this phase that the child gets the first sense of independence.

The sense of autonomy is not, of course, confined to the second and third years of life, but continues throughout childhood and early adult life. It plays a vital part in marital conflict, in the sense that spouses may marry when they still have a good deal of emotional development to undertake. In the process of their further growth they find that they have outpaced their partner, who is no longer relevant to their developed personality. This unilateral growth of one spouse is one of the major contributions to marital breakdown.

Returning now to the second and third years of life, another emotional pattern develops which is of the greatest importance. The child is learning through trial and error. It is learning to crawl by tumbling over, to stand up by falling, to handle things by breaking them. It learns to feed itself by pushing some of the food into its mouth and some onto the floor. It puts the sock on the wrong foot, etc. This is also the period when the child is testing mother's patience. Parents are not endowed with infinite patience. The time will come when mother shouts or even smacks the child, and the child also retaliates by striking back and crying. Worse, the child is shocked at experiencing mother's aggression. It also feels guilty at the pain it has caused her. Thus there is a sequence of conflict, expression of aggression, feelings of guilt and inevitably there has to be forgiveness and reparation. So, during these years, the child experiences the pain of hurting the most important source of love and feeling guilty for it. Throughout life men and women will continue to feel guilty and want to seek forgiveness when they hurt those they love. The spouse becomes such an intimate source of love, and couples experience feelings of guilt when they hurt each other.

A certain amount of conflict, anger and guilt is inevitable in any marriage: the trouble starts when one spouse begins to feel that their partner does not care sufficiently to mend their ways and is inflicting unnecessary pain. Or, having been asked repeatedly to change their ways, they make promises and then ignore them. When the spouse feels that their cries for alteration are being ignored, they then begin to feel neglected, and they cease to believe that their partner cares for them. The result is that the spouse's behaviour is attacked for its apparent callousness, as no effort is made to change in the desired way. Gradually the hurt person despairs and no longer believes that change is possible.

Fourth and Fifth Years

These are the years of the resolution of the classical oedipus complex. The little boy is expected to give up his instinctual attraction towards his mother and move in the direction of father, with the assumption of the male identity; and the same happens in reverse to the girl.

For Erikson, this is a stage of initiative when the child explores the world around it and feels in charge of life.

Erikson combines autonomy, the previous phase, with a sense of shame and doubt, and initiative with a sense of guilt. In this he is following the Freudian model. However, another characteristic which can be joined to initiative is passivity, and in marriage the passive partner can become ultimately a source of irritation to their spouse who wants them to take charge of the relationship, which they steadfastly refuse to do.

The School Years

Erikson calls the school years the phase when the child learns the sense of industry versus inferiority. But the school years are also important in the personal development of the child for another reason. Up to now the child felt loved for its own sake; not for what it achieved, but unconditionally because it existed. If this sense of unconditional love is not experienced, then the child grows up with the feeling that it only matters for what it achieves. So many men and women grow up feeling, deep inside them, unlovable as persons and consider their only worth to be their achievement. Such people feel unlovable in their own right. They enter marriage seeking love but are unable to register it because they do not know what it is to feel loved for their own sake. In the intimacy of the companionship marriage they feel bereft and unable to experience closeness. They can only offer their achievement as the sole proof of their value and can neither recognize nor register love for their personal worth.

Pathological Consequences

In the course of the description of personal growth, certain pathological consequences have been described, but more exist and, of these, *vulnerable* personalities need to be considered. Bowlby believes that the capacity to form and maintain an affectionate attachment depends on the way the parents perform their roles. Basically, when parents provide the secure basis of attachment and allow their children to explore their growing world, then these children grow up trusting, co-operative and helpful towards others. But parents can fail to do this and children can grow up without the ability to trust. These men and women, with a deep sense of insecurity, feel that those they love will let them down. They expect to be betrayed and they live with an intense feeling of insecurity, always expecting their spouse to depart. They treat their spouse as a prisoner whom they will not allow out of sight in case they have an affair. They are extremely jealous and are on the look-out for any sign of betrayal. If their spouse does have an affair, they find it very difficult to forgive and trust again. Their lack of trust makes co-operation difficult. They find it virtually impossible to believe they are wanted and so are for ever seeking fresh evidence of love. Even when the evidence is provided, they mistrust it: people are nice but don't mean it, or are nice because they want something in return.

Bowlby believes that this anxious, insecure attachment is the result of a variety of unsatisfactory parental behaviour. Thus, one or both parents may have been persistently unresponsive to the child's care-eliciting behaviour and/or actively disparaging and rejecting, or there may have been discontinuity in parenting, occurring more or less frequently, including periods in hospital or institution. Persistent threats by parents not to love a child may have been used as a means of controlling him; threats by parents to abandon the family, used as a method of disciplining the child or as a way of coercing the spouse; threats to desert or even to kill the spouse, or to commit suicide, inducing a child to feel guilty by claiming that his behaviour is or will be responsible for the parents' illness or death are other problems. These produce in the child a sense of feeling unlovable and, when as adults they form a marital relationship, they expect their spouse to abandon them in the same way as their parents threatened to do when they were children.

Karen Horney has similar attitudes to Bowlby, developed from different theoretical foundations. For her, unconditional love is essential for the child's normal development. When parents fail to give this, their children grow up without the blissful certainty of being wanted. They grow up with a basic anxiety which is described as feeling "small, insignificant, helpless, endangered in a world that is out to abuse, cheat, attack, humiliate and betray". Such feelings arise in childhood when parents fail to give warmth and affection.

Karen Horney attacked Freud's instinctual drives theory. According to her, the child not only fears punishment or desertion because of forbidden sexual drives, but because he feels the environment to be unreliable, mendacious, unappreciative, unfair, unjust, begrudging and merciless. When the child experiences his environment in this way, he feels threatened that his individuality will be obliterated, his freedom taken away and his happiness prevented. For such reasons the neurotic child has to repress his hostility (his fear of desertion, his helplessness, his need to be loved and his feelings of guilt all act to that end), and he grows up feeling that the world is a frightening and dangerous place, that he should not assert himself, that he is "bad" and that loneliness is his natural lot. Because of this natural weakness, he wishes to be protected and taken care of, puts all responsibility upon the shoulders of others, yet at the same time his suspicion of them makes it impossible to trust them. Thus he develops certain neurotic personality traits against his anxiety. These are described as affection-seeking, submissiveness, withdrawal and fear, and these patterns are seen consistently in troubled marriages.

The Neurotic Striving for Affection

Whereas in normal love the primary need is for affection, the neurotic striving for affection is based on the need for reassurance which cannot be satisfied. Such a person dislikes being alone. Sexually he or she is compulsive, and sex is a means of buying affection. They are constantly seeking reassurance but cannot believe or take it in when it is offered, though the slightest criticism or disapproval is registered. Such a person falls in and out of love frequently and may become promiscuous. When he marries he seeks constant reassurance but cannot believe that he is really loved. He is constantly waiting for the moment of rejection and when, in desperation, his partner says or does something critical, he feels that his anxious anticipation of rejection has been justified. In fact, his behaviour is often provocative, inviting rejection. He seeks love but cannot return it, and sooner or later he is abandoned by the most loving partner, who feels hopeless of ever convincing him of her love.

The Neurotic Striving for Power

Adler saw the neurotic striving for power as fundamental, but for Horney it is one of the many neurotic responses. The desire for power arises out of anxiety and feelings of inferiority. Such a person wants to overcome his fears of helplessness by feeling superior in everything. His power drive is based on hostility to others, whom he wants to disparage, frustrate and defeat. His belief is that, since he is stronger than everybody else, nobody can harm him. Such a wife or husband needs to feel always right and to be in charge. When they are obviously in the wrong, they do not apologize and, when criticized, they go to any lengths to prove their point, however misguided it may be.

Neurotic Withdrawal

This personality believes that everybody is so unreliable that the only way to survive is by becoming self-sufficient. They try to be independent of everybody. Such a wife or husband marries and then gradually withdraws into themselves except for sex. They do not exchange affection but believe they can survive on their own, a behaviour which leads to marital breakdown.

Neurotic Submissiveness

Such a personality lives for ever on the basis of fear and self-rejection. He feels that he will never have his needs met. He becomes pleasing, overhelpful and avoids criticizing. He behaves on the basis that, if he submits to the will of others, they will not hurt him in return. Such people, who always want to please, harbour a great deal of frustration and aggression underneath. They marry on the basis of pleasing but they spend their time pleasing and provoking. They appear humble on the surface yet underneath they seethe with resentment and aggression.

The dynamic theories of personality point in the direction of the need for every man and woman to grow up with the feeling of being recognized, wanted and appreciated. Many people who experience difficulties in marriage do so because they cannot feel these three things, and when they are asked about their childhood, they find it difficult to trace any marked trauma. But when one looks more closely at their upbringing, it is often found that their parents looked after them in terms of food, shelter and education, but not in respect to the growth of feelings. Such people had a childhood in which they were serviced but not loved, and in their second intimate relationship of love they do not know how to recognize or register it.

Expression of Feelings

A feature of the companionship marriage is the need to be in touch with one another, to communicate effectively. In the first intimate relationship between child and parents, communication was entered into on the basis of touch and the expression of feelings. In the second intimate experience of marriage, couples – and particularly wives – want a similar experience of communication in terms of touch and affection. The difficulty here is often encountered by men whose only physical contact is sexual and whose only form of communication is the expression of reason. There is thus often in marriage the conflict whereby the wife is in Jungian terms an intuitive, feeling person and the husband communicates in terms of intellect and reason. In practice the wife complains that her husband does not talk to her, does not express loving feelings. He is perplexed and says to her that she "knows" he loves her, he does not need to tell her so: but she does not know without active expression on his part, and so the conflict continues.

The inability to express affection is particularly important when one of the spouses is markedly starved of love. Such a wife or husband needs to have a lot of affection shown to them. They need to be shown marked recognition, the feelings of being wanted and appreciated. When the spouse expresses these positive feelings all is well, but when the partner cannot do so, then the deprived individual feels unwanted and rejected and may seek affection outside the marriage.

The inability to express angry feelings may rest on the basis of fear, the fear that if one is angry then the other person, in this case the spouse, will retaliate or reject one for good. Fear of anger resides in many people, the result of which is that they remain silent when they feel frustrated and angry; these feelings accumulate and one day burst into a mammoth explosion which takes everybody by surprise. The failure to mobilize anger may be associated with the mobilization of guilt feelings which are extremely painful.

The inability to express feelings may have a genetic basis, because men are affected more often than women, or they may be socially conditioned, or it may be the result of the child not seeing the parents express feelings to each other.

Collusion

One of the features of marital pathology recognized by the dynamic school is that of collusion (Dicks, 1967). In this pattern the couple may suit each other in terms of their social, intellectual and conscious matching of each other. But in terms of their unconscious needs they marry a person who relates to the incomplete, unexpressed or unrecognized part of themselves. For example, one often sees men and women with poor self-esteem marrying spouses who are completely suited to one another except that they do not affirm their partners. In other words, those who reject themselves unconsciously collude in marrying somebody who is rejecting. Collusion is an unconscious matching of feelings, and sooner or later spouses reach their unconscious part and then recognize that their partner is not doing justice to their needs.

Defences

In traditional psychoanalytic theory a defence is the inner, automatic inhibition of the satisfaction of an impulse that was once possible for the individual. Such an impulse generates anxiety, and defences have more commonly come to be known as the means of controlling anxiety. In the ordinary interaction of spouses, defences are used to avoid an unpleasant, painful experience. Defences include repression, which is an unconscious process of keeping down material that cannot be faced. In a similar way, there are other defences such as projection, reaction-formation, sublimation, regression, rationalization and denial. Spouses who do not wish to acknowledge an experience that is painful use one of these mechanisms to protect their feelings. Denial is a common mechanism, when the spouse claims no awareness of whatever they are accused of by their partner, or denies feelings of aggression which they are entertaining towards their spouse. The partner cannot accept that their spouse is truly unaware of the events. They accuse them of lying, and a good deal of marital counselling is required to go beyond the moral accusations which spouses fling at each other. The accusing partner has truly to appreciate that their spouse is unaware of the particular emotional experience of which the partner is trying to remind them. The same confusion can take place with projection. One partner may be harbouring aggressive feelings towards their spouse which they cannot face. They turn the tables and instead accuse the spouse of being aggressive. The exchange, "No, I am not"; "Yes, you are"; "No, I don't mean this"; "Yes, you meant it", is a familiar one between warring spouses. Sometimes, of course, spouses are simply not telling the truth, but often they are truly unaware of what they are accused of because the experience is truly unconscious. It is up to the counsellor to try to clarify what is truly deceit and what is defensive. Defences are used by people because the contents denied are threatening and anxiety-provoking. In the process of counselling, the counsellor has to help the couple reach reality by absorbing some of the anxiety and making the facing of reality possible.

Biological Basis of Personality

So far the interacting behaviour of spouses has been based on the dynamic model. The emerging personality has been considered to have been influenced by the attitude of the parents who have shaped it. The personality has also been described in different terms. Eysenck (1967) has described the human personality in terms of extroversion, introversion and neuroticism. The extrovert directs his psychic energy outwardly but tends to make superficial contact. He appears full of energy, obliging, active, with marked enthusiasm. The introvert has the opposite characteristics. His energy is inwardly directed and withdrawn from others. Extroversion is characterized by sociability, friendliness, enjoyment of excitement, talkativeness, impulsiveness, cheerfulness, activity and spontaneity. The extrovert is stimulus-hungry and expressive. The introvert is the opposite, aloof and inhibited. Neuroticism has a high anxiety element and is characterized by worrying, moodiness, tension and nervousness.

Opposites do attract and extroverts marry introverts. This interaction is often interpreted as a dominant/non-dominant relationship. The extrovert is considered to be "strong" and the introvert "weak". Marital problems arise when the extrovert person is also anxious. Under stress the extrovert succumbs and becomes full of anxiety, needing support from their spouse. Their introvert partner is taken by surprise and does not know how to respond. The extrovert suddenly breaks down into anxiety states and their introvert partner has to take charge of the relationship, something they are not accustomed to do. The ensuing strain can lead to conflict and quarrels.

Neurotic Attraction

This chapter has described the interaction of neurotic personalities which leads to marital difficulties. But do neurotic spouses attract each other? There is plenty of evidence that like marries like, or that the principle of assortative mating operates in the physical and social background of spouses (Dominian, 1980). It has been argued forcefully that assortative mating extends to neuroticism in the biological sense. That is to say, personalities with high levels of anxiety attract each other (Tharp, 1963). The studies of Kreitman (1964, 1970) have refuted this. He showed that a highly neurotic male, as measured by the Eysenck personality inventory, does not marry a spouse who has an equally high neurotic score. But after the passage of some years the non-neurotic spouse also shows a high score of anxiety. The behaviour of the neurotic husband contributes to the wife's anxiety. Such a man is dependent, emotionally irresponsible, demanding constant attention, restrictive, dominating and tends to curtail the freedom of their spouse, elevating their anxiety (Ovenstone, 1973). Kreitman's work suggests that there is no assortative mating at the biological level and he proposes instead a model of interaction. This does not mean, however, that neurotic personalities in the dynamic sense do not marry on an assortative basis as shown by the process of collusion (Dicks, 1967).

3. Presentation of Marital Problems

In Chapter 2 the dynamic and behavioural elements which might contribute to marital problems were considered. The concepts presented there unfold in the process of taking a history and counselling. But how do couples realize that they have a problem?

Start of Marital Problems

While difficulties may emerge at any time during the marriage, there is considerable evidence that the early years are frequently the period when the problems start (Dominian, 1968). A more detailed study is to be found in the book *Who Divorces?* (Thornes & Collard, 1979) from which Table 1 is taken. In a series of 520 divorced men and women, the table indicates the year in the marriage when the start of the marital problems was noted. It is clear that more than one third of the divorced believed that the problems which were to lead to divorce had started by the first anniversary of the marriage, and that by the fifth anniversary the serious difficulties had been present for 73 per cent of the sample.

Table 1

Year in the marriage and start of marital problems of a sample of 520 divorced

	All divorced n = 520	Divorced women n = 336	Divorced men n = 184
By 1st anniversary	37%	44%	23%
By 2nd anniversary	15%	15%	15%
By 3rd anniversary	9%	10%	8%
By 4th anniversary	7%	6%	8%
By 5th anniversary	5%	5%	5%
Total	73%	80%	59%

(Adapted from *Who Divorces?*, p. 119)

There are two points worth making about Table 1. The first is the very early presentation of marital difficulties and the second is the presence of gender differences. With regard to the significance of the early years, a further table in the same book indicates that, irrespective of the duration of the marriage, which may extend twenty years or more, the difficulties which were ultimately to end in divorce started within the first five years of marriage in nearly 50 per cent of cases. Thus the early years of marriage are crucial to its survival.

Gender Differences

Table 1 suggests that wives are more likely to become aware of marital problems than are their husbands. This is supported by clinical experience and by another study (Brannen & Collard, 1982) which states that "women are much more likely to say that they had recognized problems in their marriage early on, and also had defined them as such".

Nature of Complaint

Given that wives are more likely to complain, what are the most frequent behaviour patterns to which they take exception? They tend to complain about the lack of expression of affection, poor communication and dissatisfaction with sex (Brannan & Collard, 1982). As far as affection is concerned, one of the recurrent difficulties is the wife's desire to be held, stroked, caressed without necessarily leading to sex. For men affective touch is more difficult and is not easily distinguished from the early phases of sexual arousal. The same difficulty applies to communication. Women want to be talked to, to grasp what their husbands are feeling and, in return, to talk to them about their own inner world events. Husbands tend to dismiss their day's experience in a pragmatic, shorthand manner. If they talk, they tend to emphasize facts and events without embroidering them with feelings. Women on the other hand want to express their feelings, something which men mistake for gossiping or nagging.

As far as sex is concerned, wives complain that their husbands want an excess of it, whilst husbands complain that their wives are frigid because they do not want it often enough. Wives are concerned about quality and husbands about quantity. Wives feel that coitus should follow tenderness, affection and that there should be a lead-up to it. When preparation is absent, they often complain that they are treated as sexual objects. "I don't feel loved for myself, all he wants is my body" is a common complaint of wives. Husbands are fixated on the orgasm whilst wives are person-orientated. In counselling, men have to be helped to appreciate their wives as persons, and wives have to recognize the physiological, biological needs of their husbands.

The Negotiation of Difficulties

Affection, communication and sex are the most common complaints of wives, and husbands add to this list the wife's financial incompetence. These are general complaints but in addition there are an infinite number of individual ones. Whatever the complaints, how do the couples handle them? In their study Brannan & Collard (1982) come to the conclusion that there are four styles of handling complaints:

(i)   spouses attributed the difficulties to themselves or their partners;

(ii)   spouses turned a blind eye or denied there were any difficulties;

(iii) spouses attributed the difficulties to adverse or unpredictable circumstances and events extraneous to the marriage;

(iv)   spouses regarded the difficulties as transient and part of the "normal" course of events.

The commonest pattern is the one in which spouses blame one another. When couples come for counselling they will spend a great deal of time bitterly attacking the failure of each other. Sometimes the difficulties are blamed on oneself. This self-blame is often the expression of men and women who feel bad about themselves and so tend to take the whole blame for whatever has gone wrong. This is an expression of collusion. The self-rejecting partner blames himself and accepts the responsibility placed on him by his spouse who, in this way, escapes from looking at her own difficulties. For example, a man may persistently come home late from work.

Deep inside her the wife feels that this is not right; she feels unloved and unappreciated, but she does not complain. She feels that her needs are selfish and she tends to accept her husband's explanation that he works late for her sake and that of the children. In this way he escapes from recognizing that he is a workaholic who cannot leave work earlier. He needs to attend to the last minute detail because he cannot delegate.

The next way of handling difficulties is by denying that they exist. This applies in particular to husbands who refuse to accept the repeated complaint of their wives. They do not see the problem. They tend to accuse their wives of exaggerating the issues. Even worse, there are a number of occasions when the complaining wife develops symptoms of distress, such as anxiety or depression. The husband seizes the opportunity, not only to deny the existence of the problem, but also to accuse the wife, claiming that it is entirely her fault, the problem is in her imagination and she is sick. If the doctor or the counsellor is not aware of this process of projection, the wife is treated for her symptoms whilst the underlying marital problem, which belongs to both the spouses, is not examined.

The third way of dealing with marital problems is by ignoring the reality of the marital issue and instead blaming external events. These may be financial difficulties, the purchase of a house with its extra monetary stress, the loss of a job, illness and, in general, anything which might be construed as bad luck. Blaming external events for personal issues is an extremely common excuse for both spouses. The desire to escape from facing a painful emotional conflict is dealt with by rationalizing the conflict.

Finally, and up to a point in conjunction with the preceding rationalization, spouses avoid facing the seriousness of marital problems by believing that they are a temporary phase in the marriage. "Everybody has problems, we are no exception" is the ultimate utterance of this approach.

It can be seen from this complex interaction between the reality of marital problems and the interpretation of their meaning that there are several stages in the process of recognizing that there is a problem in marriage. A partner, usually the wife, may feel intuitively that something is wrong, and go through a long period of blaming herself, rationalizing the difficulty or accepting her husband's explanation that no problem exists. Brannan & Collard (1982) described this process thus: "The stage at which a person becomes aware of the existence of a possible problem in his or her marriage needs to be analytically distinguished from the stage at which he or she defined it as a marital problem, and also from the stage at which he or she decided to approach an agency."

Wives in particular become aware of marital problems early on. This awareness is not a certainty and may be dismissed on the basis of doubt or the husband's denial. But the problem keeps coming back, and at some stage the wife becomes sure that she is right. She then discusses it with her relatives and her husband. Only if this approach fails will she seek professional help, which may be from her doctor, counsellor, priest or solicitor. Sometimes spouses turn for help at a stage when they are not yet sure of their position and they seek clarification from someone who sees the matter more objectively. The health visitor, the doctor, the counsellor is asked: "Am I crazy? Have I gone off my head?", and the spouse (often the wife) has to be listened to and her anxieties ratified that something truly is seriously wrong with her marriage.

Life Events

Reference was just made to the fact that spouses may rationalize their marital difficulties through external events. They may blame, for example, the loss of their job for their marital problem. Whilst there may be no direct relationship between the loss of work and the marital difficulty – because the latter existed before and is now simply aggravated – the relationship between life events and marital difficulties has been studied. Life events assumed prominence in the psychiatric literature in the 1960s and 1970s. During these decades research workers found that critical life events – such as bereavement, loss, threat of loss, marital breakdown, etc. – are responsible for depression, anxiety and schizophrenic reactions (Briscoe, 1973; Paykel, 1969). In psychiatric literature it has been shown that critical life events may have an adverse effect and produce psychiatric illness. Brannan & Collard (1982) found in their study that those with marital problems had a fairly high incidence of critical events and problems in the eighteen-month period prior to their presentation to a marital agency.

In clinical work the presence of these critical life events is also evident. Wives lose their father or mother, on whom they have been very reliant. They may lose a child. The husband may indeed lose his job, the wife may experience her menopause or ill health, and parents may face the departure of their children. In all these cases the loss of somebody critical in the life of the spouse may mean that they need extra support, affection or help from their partner. So far they have relied on the extended family network. When someone vital to them departs, such as a beloved and supportive parent, then – at least temporarily – they need to receive more attention from their spouse. If this is available, as it usually is, the couple get closer to each other and the marital bonds are strengthened. What happens in marriage problems is that the spouse cannot mobilize the extra support. The bereaved wife or husband is now left unsupported and becomes conscious, perhaps for the first time, of how defective their spouse is. Thus the critical events put extra pressure on spouses who need an equivalent extra support from their partner. When this is missing, the stressed spouse either has suspicions of their partner's inadequacy confirmed, or becomes aware for the first time that their spouse's strength is an illusion and their reliance on it is misplaced.

Escalation of Crisis

In the end the spouse will really define that he or she has a marital problem. What are the final stages of marital discord which will make this obvious? There are four such outcomes:

(1) Persistent quarrelling
(2) Indifference
(3) Threat of departure or departure
(4) An extramarital affair

When a spouse comes to realize that something in their partner's behaviour is unacceptable, such as, for example, coming home late, drinking, flirting at parties, or that a basic need such as affection or communication is missing, then the complaint will be put forward with force. The partner may accept it and do something about it. On the other hand, he or she may steadfastly refuse either to recognize that there is a problem or to take action to change behaviour. In these circumstances the quarrels will become more frequent and bitter, and their hallmark will be a struggle without resolution of the issue. Such persistent quarrelling will be one of the reasons why couples seek help. Of course, the spouses may not seek help at all but instead go directly to a solicitor to seek divorce (Mitchell, 1981). In the midst of the quarrels, violence may be exhibited, one or both spouses may drink excessively and violence may be combined with alcohol. At this stage of severe quarrelling, spouses may leave the bedroom, sleep separately and sex may be refused. The combination of all these factors, coupled with the incessant quarrelling, usually leads to some action being taken which includes seeking help.

The alternative to quarrelling may be a deadly indifference: the spouses cease to go out together, no longer communicate with each other and do not have a sexual life. They simply coexist with a high degree of indifference to each other. This situation may last for a long time. Either partner may be frightened to leave because they cannot cope with their aloneness. They may stay together for the sake of the children. They may stay together in an empty relationship for religious reasons. But the relationship is highly unstable, and the departure of children, the arrival of another man or woman, or the support gained from counselling may alter the situation and cause the partners to go their separate ways.

In fact, either the escalating quarrel or the indifference may lead one spouse to threaten to leave or actually to go. Short interval departures act as one of the critical mechanisms to make the spouse take notice that a serious problem exists. Frequent separations are related to highly unstable marriages. When the separation becomes prolonged, then the chances of reconciliation become less. In an American study (Bloom, 1977), it was shown that the likelihood of any married couple experiencing a separation was found to be nearly 5 per cent in one year. Most separations after lasting a year end in divorce.

Although sexual liberality has increased in the last twenty-five years, the presence of an affair is the sign that the marriage is under threat. There are, of course, at least two types of affairs. The first is the casual experience of intercourse which is not meant to be taken seriously and does not threaten the marriage. Men who travel and are alone may have a transient affair, a one-night stand, which in most cases their wives know nothing about.

There is a second variety of affair in which either spouse is deeply engaged in an extramarital relationship which becomes known to their partner. This type of affair is often interpreted as threatening the vital security of the marriage and is expected to be abandoned. When an affair of the second type is discovered, couples may deal with it themselves, seek help or declare the marriage at an end and seek divorce.

Health Problems

The presence of persistent marital difficulties may lead to physical or psychological symptoms. In a study of neurotic illness in several general urban practices, marital problems were the factors most associated with minor psychiatric illness (Shepherd, 1966). The psychiatric symptoms prior to marital breakdown are those of anxiety and depression. Couples experience breathlessness, palpitations, sweating, different forms of fears, pain in the chest, abdominal pains, feelings of nausea, hot and cold feelings, backache, insomnia, tiredness, a sense of misery, and lethargy; in the more severe forms, there may be suicidal attempts (Kessel, 1965; Bancroft, 1977). Clearly the general practitioner should be alert to the likelihood of a marital difficulty in the presence of these symptoms. In the course of taking a history, a routine question of "How are things at home?" should extract a rapid response which will illuminate the underlying marital problems.

Agency of Referral

When couples seek help, they are more likely to go to their doctor if they can present themselves with a physical symptom. Their presence in the doctor's surgery will then become respectable. Very often they use their physical symptoms to seek help for their underlying marital problem and – as already mentioned – this is only likely to be forthcoming if their doctor makes the correct diagnosis. Brannen & Collard (1982) showed in their study that respondents with marital problems who nevertheless had predominantly medical symptoms, were likely to appear at a medical agency, whereas those who experienced marital problems in terms of conflict, indifference, separation, threatened separation or extramarital affairs were likely to go to a marriage guidance agency.

Section 2

4. Early Years of Marriage

Marital Breakdown in the Early Years

As has been already indicated, the early years of marriage are particularly prone to marital difficulties. A study going back to the fifties showed that nearly 50 per cent of the married sample interviewed had adjustment difficulties (Pierce, 1963). Subsequent work has confirmed the vulnerability of the early years. One study found that 38 per cent of divorcees had ceased to cohabit by their fifth anniversary, but only 16 per cent had divorced by this period (Chester, 1971). The period during which couples live together is shorter than the legal duration of the marriage. It is called the De Facto duration as against the De Jure, which is the legal period. Official statistics of divorce refer to the De Jure period and tend to underestimate the vulnerability of the early years, in which the first five years seem crucial. One of the reasons why there is a delay of divorce in the early years is the fact that, until 1984, couples could not petition for early divorce, having to wait for three years except in exceptional circumstances. This part of the 1971 Act has now been repealed and couples can seek divorce after one year. The new law, the Matrimonial and Family Proceedings Act 1984, will make the separation of the couple and their divorce come closer to each other.

Table 1

Divorce by duration of marriage in Great Britain (percentage)							
	Duration of marriage (complete years)						
	0–2	3–4	5–9	10–14	15–19	20–24	25–29	30+
Year of divorce 1983	1.3	19.5	28.7	19.2	12.9	8.6	5.2	4.7

If we look at Table 1 we find that of all divorces 49.5 per cent had taken place by the ninth year of marriage (*Social Trends*, 1985). Since the mean delay between separation (i.e. the De Facto duration of marriage) and divorce has been variously calculated as 4.6 years (Chester, 1972), 5 years from magistrate court action to divorce (McGregor, 1970), and 5.2 years from separation to divorce (Thornes & Collard, 1979), this tends to confirm the early separation of nearly 50 per cent of divorces. This fact shows that support for the early years of marriage is a crucial aspect of the drive to prevent marital breakdown.

Schema for Examining Marital Problems in the Early Years

Given that the early years are so crucial to the survival of marriage, is there any scheme by which the marriage can be examined meaningfully, in addition to the general dynamic and behavioural considerations already outlined in Chapter two? Such a scheme has been proposed (Dominian, 1980) in which the social, emotional, sexual, intellectual and spiritual dimensions of a marital relationship are considered. When listening to a couple's story, attention is focused on one or more of these areas, which in turn is reinforced during the counselling. Furthermore, when a couple or an individual finds it difficult to describe their marriage, the helping agent can actually question the person about these areas. In this way the therapist can become aware in the shortest possible time of the problems causing difficulties.

Social
Family Network

The most important aspect of the social life of the spouses is the attitude of the parents to the impending partner and the developing relationship of spouses with their parents after the marriage. The support of the family means that the partners will continue to have the goodwill and assistance of their parents. This is particularly important in the relationship between the wife and her mother, but the general encouragement and advice of parents is important to both spouses. There is evidence (Thornes & Collard, 1979) to indicate that those who divorce belong to a group of marriages which were opposed by the parents.

After the wedding the partner becomes the most significant person in the life of the spouse. It is usual for a mature couple to reach the stage of development when, by the time they get married, they have outgrown their emotional dependence on their parents. This, in fact, applies to the vast majority of men and women. But there are some who get married and still cling to their parents. Such spouses will insist on visiting them excessively, on listening to their advice – which amounts to running the spouse's life – and, when a problem arises, they bypass their partner and go directly to one parent for help. This is, of course, resented by the other spouse, who feels ignored. Thus daughters may remain tied to their mother's apron strings; sons may continue to work with their father, who remains the "boss" in every aspect of their life. Wives may be on the telephone continuously to their mothers and refuse to act without the latter's consent and advice. Clearly such spouses produce problems for their partner, who feels he comes second to the spouse's family. This is resented and fought against. The outcome of the fight depends on the possibility of maturity of the emotionally dependent partner. Can they stand on their own two feet? Can they shift their attention from their parents and relatives to the spouse? Can they use their partner as the main source of communication? The outcome of the marriage will depend on how much the ignored partner minds playing a passive role, and how quickly the dependent partner can grow up and no longer need to lean on parents. Sometimes both spouses are dependent on their families and refuse to give them up. This results in a continuous test of strength as to which family's advice will prevail.

Both in-laws, but particularly mothers-in-law, provide problems early in marriage (Blood & Wolfe, 1960). The mother may be emotionally dependent on her son, idolize him, be unwilling to see him get married and consequently refuse to accept his choice. Every girl he brings home will be found unsatisfactory. When finally he marries someone of his choice, she will be constantly criticized. If the husband has an argument with the detested wife, his mother will take his side. In fact she will do all she can to blacken the image of her daughter-in-law. If the couple have serious marital difficulties, she will encourage a break-up of the marriage and welcome her son back home. The same, of course, applies to a close mother-daughter relationship.

A different mother-in-law problem occurs when the wife and mother-in-law have to share the same household. This is not unusual in some ethnic groups. The newly wedded wife may have to bow to the wishes of her mother-in-law who remains the senior and dominant person in the household.

The spouses have not only to separate from their intimate connection with their parents and make each other the central figure in their lives, but also to leave behind some friends of significance, particularly their former boy or girl friends. Clearly some friends of each partner will be integrated into the new social network of the marriage. But sometimes trouble begins very early in the marriage for two reasons. The first is that the wife or husband still insists on maintaining close ties with a previous boy or girl friend. This inevitably leads to a jealous response on the part of the spouse, and to many quarrels. The second problem is also that of jealousy, but now based on the pathology of the spouse. He or she cannot accept that their partner had a previous intimate relationship. They question their partner endlessly. They want to find out the most minute details about their character and personality, and are obsessed with the previous sexual behaviour. Such obsessional preoccupation with the past may lead to constant interrogation, keeping the partner up in the late hours of the night, finding out in the most detailed way about the conduct of those they have replaced. Such spouses are extremely anxious about their own emotional hold over their partner and about their own sexual performance. They compare themselves unfavourably with others in both respects and yearn to be reassured that their partner will not leave them or compare them harshly with previous lovers. In desperation, spouses not only reveal the truth about their previous lives but, under pressure, may elaborate details which did not exist. Their jealous spouse may note inconsistencies in their accounts and accuse them of lying. Such a jealousy of the past is rarely free from jealousy of the present. Wives will become violently aggressive if their partner looks at or flirts with another woman.

This type of jealousy, as already indicated, is an expression of a very insecure personality who feels constantly threatened that they will be found out, declared "no good" and abandoned. They seek constant reassurance but, in the end, they push their partner to a point beyond endurance and the marriage breaks down.

Setting Up Home

Having negotiated the hurdle of separation from parents, making the marriage the key relationship and yet remaining friendly with parents, relatives and friends, the next immediate challenge is for the couple to set up home. An independent home is achieved more often by the higher socio-economic groups and those who marry after the age of 20 (Ineichen, 1977). Those who eventually divorce are more likely to share households and not to possess a home of their own in the early years (Thornes & Collard, 1979).

Possessing a home of one's own means that the couple are free to experiment, find out by their mistakes, express their affection freely and without apprehension of being watched, and participate in a sexual life which is not threatened by a curious audience. It has therefore enormous advantages.

After a home of one's own is achieved, there follows the process of running it. Currently there is a belief that men are more prone to contribute to household tasks than before, and in general this is the case, but work being carried out on the early years of marriage at the Marriage Research Centre by P. Mansfield indicates that husbands are not contributing as much to the management of the home as the popular notion would suggest. In fact, newly wedded wives are still expected to work and to look after the home. This can lead to conflict, as the husband may have given different expectations at the time of the courtship.

But the contribution of the husband is assessed particularly at times of excessive stress on the wife – when she has more to do at work, becomes ill, is preoccupied with a sick relative or especially when children arrive. It is at times of stress that she needs to rely on her husband, and his willingness to help at such times is crucial to his image in the household.

Money

Money frequently appears as an issue in matrimonial disputes. The complaints are usually twofold. Firstly, one spouse, often the wife, complains that her husband is mean and expects her to run the home on a minimum budget; secondly, that the money is misspent. This is usually the husband's view, namely that his wife is a spendthrift or incompetent. Every financial charge and countercharge has to be examined objectively. When wives complain of meanness, the actual amount given should be ascertained so that a realistic view can be taken of the complaint. Sometimes it is true that the husband expects to get away with an insufficient amount and, at other times, it is the wife who cannot manage on a generous allowance. Wives complain bitterly when they are kept short of money for the house but the husband spends a good deal on cigarettes, drink or gambling, or maintains relatives.

What has also to be remembered is that money is a highly symbolic entity. It often stands as a proof of the affection of the spouse. "If he loved me, he would not keep me short or make me ask repeatedly for money." Another aspect of money is the freedom that it gives to the owner.

One of the many reasons why women feel so much more free in marriage today is that many of them work and so have some independent means separately from their husband. Frequently their income is given over to the family and very little is kept for themselves, but at least in principle wives are not so dependent on their husband's goodwill for survival.

Of course, at the beginning of marriage and before the

children arrive, it is likely that both spouses will be working and that money may not be a frequent problem. That will come later when the wife has no income. At this stage the argument may be both about the money available to the wife and her access to it. When she worked a wife had an income of her own or control over her wages. When she ceased working, she probably lost access to draw freely and became dependent upon her husband's whim.

Leisure

One of the most frequent complaints early in marriage is made by wives who are deeply resentful of the fact that their husbands have married them but continue to act as though they are bachelors. Thus a man may marry, yet spend all his leisure time with his friends playing sport or drinking in the pub. He may bring his wife to these activities but pay no attention to her whilst otherwise engaged. This type of man appears to enjoy the advantages of marriage – such as a home, food and sex – but does not consider he is under any obligation to be available to his wife. Occasionally, as mentioned already, he spends all his spare time with his parents or alternatively with his friends. Sometimes the wife is left entirely at home, and her need for companionship totally ignored. Closeness in the early years of marriage is a vital element of modern marriage, and its absence leaves the wife feeling neglected and abandoned.

Sometimes the wife wants her husband to do things in the home. Husbands usually oblige but there are some who have the habit of promising and never starting, or starting and never finishing. Wives bitterly complain of incomplete kitchens, bedrooms and sitting rooms, repairs of which go on for months or years. The same feeling is aroused: "If you loved me, you would not make excuses but you would finish the job." The inability to finish the work is not infrequently coupled with a willingness to do all sorts of work for neighbours or others whilst the tasks at home are left incomplete. This type of husband may be the sort of person who wants to please, finds it difficult to say No and so keeps obliging everybody except his wife, towards whom he feels free to say No. Occasionally the relationship between spouses has become so hostile that the delay in completing household tasks is a way of "punishing" the wife.

Work

The difficulties described for leisure apply also to work. This, of course, concerns those who start their married life with employment, and particularly the upper- and middle-class groups. At the beginning of the marriage both spouses are likely to be employed but whilst the wife has a young child she often drops out of work, at least temporarily. Husbands who work usually finish in time to get home and spend the evening and weekend with their wife and children. There are a few people, however, who put their business before their marriage. These are mostly men – and a few women – who work all hours of the day and night. They come home late, bring work home, work at the weekends and once again want to enjoy the pleasures of marriage whilst putting all their energies into their work. Such men are often extrovert, bubbling with energy and enthusiasm, who find their work all-consuming and ignore anything or anybody else. Wives of such men feel ignored and neglected and may protest loudly at their husband's behaviour. The husband in turn may rationalize it all by saying he is doing it for her and the children, and in this way an impasse follows. Life is about a balance between work and personal relationship and, if the latter is ignored, then the marriage is imperilled.

Health

The early years of marriage, before the arrival of the children, are a necessary time for the spouses to get to know each other. During these critical years illness may intervene. The role of illness at this time has not been examined in detail, but its presence is found recurrently in the histories of marital difficulties. Spouses may be incapacitated for a period of months or sometimes years through a physical illness, operation, accident or a combination of more than one factor. During all this time, the spouse acts as a devoted nurse, and has no sexual relationship. The time comes when the illness is over and the couple want to resume their marital life, particularly the sexual activity, but find they cannot. Without realizing it, their relationship has become that of brother and sister. During the illness they become attached to each other as friends rather than as sexual beings and, when they want to return to the man-woman relationship, they find this very difficult.

The same difficulty may apply when a nurse marries a patient, or when two patients in a psychiatric unit marry. Often these relationships work out satisfactorily, but sometimes the attraction was really based on the availability of the carer rather than the man-woman relationship and so, after the wedding, the affection remains but the sexual attraction is absent.

The husband or wife may not be ill continuously but at frequent intervals during these early years. The attention that should be channelled into getting to know each other is spent in recovering from the ailment. Invariably such concentration on survival means that energy for affection and sex is reduced or absent. The healthy spouse comes to be conditioned to illness and not to a healthy spouse and, when health finally does appear, finds it difficult to respond The partner is tuned in to self-control and absence of affection, so that he or she comes to learn to live without tenderness or sex. In a sense both have been removed from the range of possibility, and when the situation changes it is not possible to bring these needs to the forefront.

Emotional Aspects of the Personality
Freedom

One of the distinguishing characteristics of the single person is their freedom. They are accountable in their work to their superiors, but in their personal lives are answerable only to themselves. This freedom is curtailed in marriage. Spouses have to take account of each other's needs, characteristics and wishes, and they have to shape their own lives in terms not only of their own wishes but also of those of their partner. Most couples achieve this. But at the beginning of marriage some spouses may have special difficulties in this area. These are men and women who are extremely sensitive to any restriction of their freedom, interpreting a request on their time as such a restriction and as a demand. They feel hemmed in and are constantly coming home late, going out without notifying their partner and taking action without consultation. This sensitivity misinterprets the intentions of their spouse, who is often felt to be almost a jailer, without any good reason. On such a sensitive person any restriction is interpreted as an imposition, any request as an order. The spouse retaliates by getting angry, and quarrels follow at frequent intervals.

When both partners are sensitive and want their independence, then the quarrels escalate. Each watches the other with the suspicion that they are about to impose their will. The spouse is experienced as a restrictive parent. In clinical practice this pattern is seen when two rebellious young people leave home to gain their independence. They cohabit or marry. Having got their freedom from home, they are not, of course, prepared to accept any restrictions from each other, and the unity assembled to fight the parents fragments as they fight each other.

The natural thing for any person who feels restricted in their relationship is to work out a balance between freedom and the need to accommodate their partner. When this is not possible, going their separate ways is the only alternative. But this may not be easy, because often their intense quest for independence is coupled with an equivalent degree of emotional dependence. They want to be free but they cling to the support they get from each other, which often leads to an aggressive stalemate of feeling trapped.

Dominance

The word "dominance" appears frequently in the social and psychological literature. It is not easy to define its meaning accurately. In terms of the marital relationship it describes a person who appears emotionally strong, decisive, clear, precise, eager to exercise control, finds it difficult to accept criticism, does not tolerate contradiction, likes to have his own way and is authoritarian. Such a person can be either spouse but is often the husband.

He is in control of his home, wife and children. He commands obedience, requires his wishes to be met and expects things to be done his way. On the surface this is a picture of strength, order and precision. The wife may accept being treated in this way for a while – even enjoy it and rebel later on – but many object from the very start of the marriage. In that case there are immense and bloody battles. The wife refuses to obey her husband's commands and goes her own way. He tries to stop her, and to restrict her activities and freedom. If he has any hold over her, such as a financial one, he uses it to control her.

A wife describes this type of husband this way: "He is impossible. He wants to have everything his way. He comes home and acts like a sergeant-major. He barks and wants to inspect. Of course I can never please him. There is something wrong with everything I do. The food is too hot or too cold. The house is dirty or the floor is slippery. My friends are no good; in fact he hasn't got a good word for anybody. If I try to please him, I get 'no, thank you'. He says it is my duty to look after him. That's what women are for. Mind you, I can understand his thinking when I see how his dad treats his wife, like a bit of dirt. But he will not treat me like that. I swear to that."

Such a wife may in fact rebel, pack her bags and go. The dominant person should, in theory, let her go and carry on with his life as if he did not need her. Sometimes this is what happens, but often a surprise follows. The so-called strong man becomes desperately anxious at his wife's departure. He cannot survive on his own. He looks for her everywhere. When he finds her he pleads, often on his knees, for her to return. He makes all sorts of promises to change. Sometimes he does change, but often the wife returns and the situation soon returns to its previous condition.

This person differs from the emotionally mature, confident, resilient man who gives the appearance of strength and is in fact able to cope with problems and anxiety in an effective way. Such a person does not need to control, dominate or exercise power over others. He is content to be available in a reliable way to his wife.

Dependence

What sort of woman marries a dominant man? In practice it is often found that such a woman has features of dependence.

Once again, dependence is difficult to define. But it embraces a child-like need to hold on to an authoritarian, parental figure. The dependent person has not outgrown their need to be taken care of, to lean on others, to have their minds made up for them and to be guided; since they are often over-anxious, they need someone to tell them what to do so that their anxiety can be reduced.

The dependent wife may tolerate a dominant man who is prepared to run her life for her. At a later stage, when she finds her maturity, she may find such dominance unacceptable and, as will be shown in Chapter 7, emotional growth from dependence to independence accounts for a vast amount of marital breakdown.

Another feature of the dependent personality which is not at all well recognized is their self-abasement. Such a man or woman may find it very difficult to believe that anybody wants, appreciates or loves them. They are prepared to be dominated or even controlled, for in this way they feel accepted. They reckon they deserve nothing better and are fortunate to have anyone marrying them. At the beginning such men and women feel flattered that they have been selected by their spouse. They are prepared to pay the price of accepting their spouse's dominance, and will do anything so long as they feel accepted. But little by little this self-rejection will be questioned, and they will require better treatment, which if not forthcoming may lead to marital breakdown.

Unreliability

Some marriages come to a halt very early on. A wife may marry a man who is soon found to be unreliable. She may discover he does not open his letters, does not pay his bills, wants her to organize his life and attend to the practicalities of the home whilst he opts out from responsibility. When a difficulty arises he hands it over to her; when pushed to act he makes excuses. This pattern of unreliability may persist for many years with the wife patiently tolerating it. She may be very willing to run his life for him.

But if she herself is anxious and insecure, then her spouse's behaviour is too much of a problem. She needs to feel she can trust her husband and rely on his ability to handle routine matters. If this is not forthcoming, she may find the anxiety too much and she simply departs.

Unreliability may be part of a psychopathic syndrome characterized by insecurity, inability to relate, aggression and violence. Such people have a long history of instability in their lives which they continue in the marriage, which rarely lasts.

Apathy

Another pattern of early dissolution is the marriage in which a husband or wife does not really want to get married but drifts into it. Usually such a marriage has been preceded by a courtship of long duration in which one spouse wants to get married and the other does not. Finally the reluctant partner gives in, through social and family pressure, and consents to marry. The marriage is an empty affair. The reluctance to stay married returns and the couple find they are not sharing a social, affectionate or sexual life. Their relationship simply peters out.

Quarrelling

In the presence of these difficulties most spouses will quarrel: but not all couples will do so. Some may have seen a lot of conflict in their homes and refuse to repeat the pattern. The non-quarrelling partners may simply leave one another without having exchanged one nasty word.

But most couples quarrel. A quarrel is an expression of anger against the partner and results in a retaliation. In this way the partners inform one another that there is something wrong and that they have been hurt. Usually the message of anger and pain is sufficient to change that particular course of behaviour.

A smaller group of couples quarrel, not so much with the purpose of clarifying the issue but in order to hurt one another. This is an embittered battle where hurting and punishing are the order of the day.

Other spouses get angry but do not let their anger out. They let it accumulate and then one day they explode. Still others get angry easily but not deeply. They have their say and forget about it within minutes. They do not harbour a grudge. Others do, having long memories and not letting their spouses forget their misdeeds. The frequent reminder of their faults is a form of nagging which enters the clinically combative relationship.

Most couples quarrel and then make up. There are a few men and women who cannot relax after an argument. They cannot tolerate closeness and, if their spouse approaches them to make it up, they push them away. They want to be left alone to get over their hurt and anger. Sometimes this may take days and even weeks as they sulk silently.

Sexual Problems

In Thornes & Collard's (1979) book there is a table which gives percentages of sexual satisfaction at the start of marriage, and these are quoted in Table 2.

Table 2

Sexual satisfaction at the start of marriage (percentage)

	Divorced women	Continuous married women	Divorced men	Continuous married men
	n = 336	n = 371	n = 184	n = 199
Satisfactory	76	85	84	94
Not satisfactory	24	15	15	6

Table 2 shows that 24 per cent of divorced women find their sexual life unsatisfactory at the start of their marriage, compared to 15 per cent of continuously married women, and 15 per cent of divorced men, compared to 6 per cent of continuous married men. Thus both divorced and non-divorced spouses have problems, but the divorced women and men have a higher incidence and, unlike those who stay married, their problems do not improve with time.

Further analysis of the dissatisfaction showed that divorced husbands and wives had different complaints about each other. Women complained that their husbands were "selfish" and "cruel", whereas men described their wives as "cold". Another distinction, this time between divorced and continuously married, was that the former attributed their problem to the fault of their partner, whereas those married accepted mutual responsibility, seeing it was their common problem to be worked out, rather than blaming each other.

Studies by Bauer (1983) have shown that low interest in sex and lack of enjoyment are the commonest experiences of women who have sexual difficulties. Lack of enjoyment includes also absence of, or difficulty in having, an orgasm. A less common reason is painful intercourse. These problems are associated with physical and psychological causes. As far as the latter are concerned, anxiety and anger play a prominent part.

The anxiety of being hurt is a straightforward fear, but anxiety may accompany ignorance, apprehension of coitus, religious taboos, the feeling that sex is dirty and the fear of pregnancy. In Fisher's study (1973) of the female orgasm, he found that the fear of being abandoned and a detached relationship with the father were present. Reference has been made to lack of self-esteem, and the woman who feels unlovable cannot respond easily to being loved sexually.

Anger with the spouse is a self-evident reason for avoidance of coitus. Usually the anger is transient but in some relationships it becomes a constant presence, in which case sex may be interrupted on a more permanent basis. In the angry scenes, often described in marriage counselling, spouses may leave their marital bed and sleep elsewhere. They return only to encounter the same attitudes, which lead to further withdrawals and so vicious circles are established.

A common feature of pathological sexuality early in marriage is the sexual relationship which was satisfactory during courtship or cohabitation, but which disappears when the couple get married. A woman doctor put the problem thus: "I pursued my boyfriend relentlessly. I wanted to sleep with him on every possible occasion. When he agreed to marry me, I switched off. It is as if the moment he agreed, I had him in my power and I did not want him any more. We married and I went right off sex. I went to see a sexual therapist but it was no good. I no longer fancied my husband. But there is nothing wrong with my sexual function. I am having an affair and I am enjoying sex."

The switching off of sexual desire in marriage, after intensively successful premarital coitus, is a difficult problem to explain. The explanation is likely to be psychological in nature. In some cases there is the element of wanting to be loved and a chase. So long as the person is chasing for recognition all is well. The moment they are acknowledged on a permanent basis in marriage they lose their interest. This is suggestive of impaired personalities who want desperately to feel wanted and to be enjoyed. As long as they are seeking this response their inhibitions are suppressed, but when they are rewarded on a permanent basis they cannot accept the love. They feel they don't deserve it, which often goes with poor self-esteem. They are afraid to trust themselves and now they entertain the danger of being abandoned. They use their body for the sexual chase but do not believe that their spouse appreciates the very same body when they get married. In other cases the chase is carried out by a woman who is socially and intellectually adult but emotionally still a child. As a child they are seeking affection but when this is given sexually in marriage they become anxious at the thought that a little girl is marrying an adult, often a father figure, with whom sexual intercourse is impossible. All these "explanations" are dynamic conjectures. The person is unconscious of the reasons for their behaviour; all they know is that they are no longer interested in sex.

Sexual Dysfunction

Amongst the sexual dysfunctions men frequently suffer from erectile impotence and premature ejaculation, and women from dyspareunia and vaginismus. All these may be present at the beginning of marriage and need detailed investigation. The commonest dysfunction of the early years is non-consummation. In this condition the woman finds penetration too painful and pushes the husband away. The husband is usually a gentle, unforceful man who does not want to hurt his wife and so desists from intercourse. The couple may not have coitus for some time, until relatives and friends begin to ask questions about children. It is this which brings them to their doctor.

Sexual Variations

Men have numerous fetishes and may like their wives to wear fur, rubber, black underclothes, high heels and many other variations, including cross-dressing. These variations are not at this stage likely causes of marital breakdown. There is, however, one exception and that is homosexuality. Most homosexuals do not marry but a few do, and some of these find, very soon after their marriage, that they cannot continue with sexual intercourse or indeed with the marriage.

Extramarital Intercourse

Extramarital intercourse in the early years of marriage is not common. Eysenck (1978) postulates that the stable extrovert with high libido and the unstable introvert who finds it difficult to establish regular relationships with the opposite sex, are both likely to have extramarital intercourse. In both these cases intercourse is often an isolated and transient experience. The spouse does not know about it and there is no threat to the marriage. On the other hand, early and continuous dissatisfaction with the marriage may lead to alternative relationships. One such dissatisfaction has been mentioned already, that is the situation when one partner goes off sex after marriage and has an affair to test their sexual attractiveness.

When a spouse finds out about the affair of their partner, they may be angry initially but accept it as a joint responsibility and try to understand their own part in pushing their spouse to have an affair. On the other hand the affair may not be approached in this way, and the guilty spouse may be blamed totally for his or her behaviour. It is rare for one affair actually to bring the marriage to an end, but it erodes the trust that exists between the spouses.

Intellectual

There is considerable evidence that as far as physical and social factors are concerned there is a tendency towards assortative mating, that is to say like marries like (Coleman, 1977). There is a good likelihood that at marriage men and women will match each other on age, education and intelligence. This type of similarity tends to ensure that spouses are capable of pursuing common intellectual interests and sharing some of them. They are capable of talking to one another in a language that is understood and of exchanging ideas that are of mutual interest. Such a common approach to life obviously ensures that the bonding at the emotional and sexual level is reinforced further intellectually.

Rarely this does not happen. Couples will marry after a hasty courtship, knowing very little about each other. In these marriages – which in the past have often been precipitated by premarital pregnancy – the reasons for marriage are extraneous to the mutual attraction. One or both spouses may be desperate to get married and will accelerate a slight acquaintance into matrimony. The encounter may be no more than a physical infatuation. Pressure may be exerted by one or both families. One spouse may elicit the sympathy and compassion of the other, without a proper process of courtship.

Whatever the reason, such hasty and ill-conceived marriages may work for a short period and then the couple discover that they have little in common. They cannot speak to one another, they have little of common interest, and a sense of boredom descends on the relationship which envelops the emotional and sexual side as well. The prospect for such marriages is poor and they are unlikely to last beyond the first five years.

Spiritual

Generally religion plays a very small part in the motivation for marriage. Marriages continue to be solemnized in church, although the proportion has fallen recently overall to one half (Haskey, 1980). But church weddings remain high where the marriage is the first for both parties. In fact in 1978 the manner of solemnization was religious in 88.5 per cent of cases when the couple were bachelor and spinster.

But a religious solemnization is no indication of the fervour of religious values. Most often the service is a social event with no particular religious significance for married life later on.

Nevertheless, there is evidence that strength of religious feeling can be a strong association (Coleman, 1977) and, as might be expected, this reflects church attendance. When both partners are regular church attenders, then the assortative factor is high and, of course, in this situation it has implications later for the married life of the couple. In the study of Thornes & Collard (1979) there is support for the assumption that when partners are churchgoers this is a factor which is associated with marital stability.

In the past when denominational attitudes were more sharply delineated, mixed religious marriages were considered a risk for marital breakdown (Dominian, 1968). But the ecumenical atmosphere of recent times has both softened and relaxed this attitude, and the mixing of religions is not likely to be a provocative factor in marital breakdown, except in rare instances where the religious beliefs held are extreme.

In the absence of strong actual religious beliefs, spouses may hold other strong values, which are their particular expressions of faith. Here the couple may have divergent views, which may lead to conflict. Either partner may wish to have children, whilst the other wants to pursue a career free from obligations to a family. One spouse may seek wealth and power whilst the other wants to pursue traditional expectations of children and family life. One spouse may want an intense social life whilst the other rejoices in staying at home. In these situations couples may become disenchanted with each other's values and priorities, to the point where they do not wish to continue the relationship.

5. Childbearing

One of the principal reasons for marriage is to have children, and to educate and help them to become mature citizens. Children in turn need stable marriages within which to develop and realize their potential. This book does not deal with the impact of marital breakdown on children, which is a subject on its own, but this chapter examines the effect of childbearing on marriage, from conception to the arrival of the baby. Most of the material is taken from clinical experience supported, wherever possible, by factual information.

Live Births

Table 1 shows that the number of live births has been falling consistently since 1961, with a slight break in 1981. In particular, numbers of second and third children have shown a substantial fall. At present large families are not in favour. As far as marital breakdown is concerned, there is evidence that the physical and mental ill-health increases with family size, a critical point being reached with four children or more (Hare & Shaw, 1965). Since health plays a major part in marital relationships, the reduction in family size may be advantageous and in favour of marital stability. Indeed, recent work shows an association between marital breakdown and a large family (Murphy, 1984; Thornes & Collard, 1979).

Table 1

Live births (thousands)

	1961	1971	1976	1981	1982	1983
Legitimate live births to women married once only						
First	278	280	211	215	202	201
Second	229	235	195	193	188	183
Third	121	107	64	73	72	71
Fourth	58	43	20	22	23	22
Fifth or later	61	33	13	12	12	13
Total	747	698	503	515	497	490
Total illegitimate live births	48	66	54	81	90	99

(Table adapted from *Social Trends*, 1985)

The proportion of illegitimate births continues to rise, and in 1983 some 16 per cent of all births in England and Wales were illegitimate. Illegitimacy is a complex phenomenon, but once again it should be noted that, increasingly, single women who become pregnant do not marry on account of the baby, and so one contribution to marital breakdown is reduced, namely that of marriages related to a premarital pregnancy. There has been an increase of joint registration by parents from 46 per cent in 1972 to nearly 60 per cent in 1982, suggesting that, although they do not get married before the birth of the child, single women are likely to have maintained a good relationship with the father outside marriage (*Social Trends*, 1985).

Childlessness

At the other end of the scale there are the marriages with no children. The reasons for not having children are physiological, due to a variety of male and female infertility, and psychological, including non-consummation, the unwillingness to parent and the fragility of the marriage which cautions the spouses against childbearing. Indeed, there is considerable evidence associating childlessness with divorce both in Britain (Rowntree, 1964; Thornes & Collard, 1979) and in the U.S.A. (Jacobson, 1950). This view has been challenged by several authors including Chester (1972). However, further analysis (Murphy, 1984) has confirmed the finding. The absence of a child may, as already suggested, indicate that the marriage finds itself in difficulties from the very start through social, emotional or sexual incompatibility, and the couple separate before conception. The parties may be emotionally threatened by the possibility of a child. Clinically one sees partners who are emotionally mutually very dependent and cannot contemplate the dilution of the attention they receive from each other. At a later stage people may mature unilaterally, leave the marriage, remarry and have a child. Childless couples include wives who are keen on a career and do not wish to have children. Later on the career becomes supremely important and replaces the marriage.

The history of those who experience marital difficulties often contains an account of the stressful process of infertility investigations. These consist of embarrassing and painful examinations for the wife and an investigation of the husband's semen. The fact that the couple cannot conceive when they want to is a shock, an attack on their masculinity and femininity. Their friends are having babies and they cannot. Often there are no physical reasons to explain the infertility, and the couple interpret the negative findings as their fault. They are told they are stressed and have to relax, and this often activates further anxiety.

The desire to have a baby may become intense, and recent events of in vitro fertilization and surrogate motherhood, have shown to what lengths couples are prepared to go to achieve this. But the drama of in vitro fertilization hides the tension that the ordinary steps in overcoming fertility produce. The earliest treatment is to identify ovulation through temperature charting and to have intercourse at the appropriate time prior to or during ovulation. This usually means months of careful temperature taking. As period time approaches, there is a heightening of tension regarding the outcome. When the period arrives, it is met with deep disappointment and the process starts all over again.

During this phase of waiting there is an inevitable disturbance of affection and sexual life. Coitus ceases to be a normal expression of love and becomes a purely biological act with a single target in mind, namely the fusion of ovum and sperm. Spontaneity recedes as the couple have to abstain on the infertile days and have intercourse on certain nights only. Sex loses its vitality and, if the process lasts for a long time, this produces subtle changes of attitude to intercourse, which becomes devoid of its natural meaning. Affection can also recede as the couple concentrate on reproduction. Over time the effort put into having a child erodes the energy available for maintaining the marriage.

Finally, conception takes place and at once the pregnancy becomes precious and associated with considerable anxiety. Everything fades before the importance of ensuring that nothing goes wrong. The significance of the husband is diminished compared to the importance of the unborn baby. Sexual intercourse may be stopped in case it harms the foetus: and so, for nine months, the unborn life dominates the scene.

Then the baby arrives and, if care is not taken, it may dominate the life of the family. So much effort has gone into its creation that this has to be continued in the early years of its life, once more at the expense of the husband.

Clearly all these behaviour reactions are possibilities which do not necessarily occur in every instance, but they are all possibilities which have to be guarded against. Sometimes the process is interrupted by a spontaneous abortion or a stillbirth, and then life becomes complicated indeed.

During infertility the emotional reaction of the spouses is vital. So often the couple not only feel embarrassed at their inability to conceive but this can also be interpreted as a general ineptitude. Self-esteem is lowered, and gradually both partners feel unworthy of each other's love. They feel failures and wonder why the other chose them at all. The woman in particular may suffer if she equates femininity with motherhood.

In practice all this means that a pregnancy achieved against a background of infertility has to be helped not only to overcome the normal anxieties about its well-being but also to ensure that the marital relationship is not suffering. The couple have to be encouraged to feel that the infertility is not their fault, and thus reduce the sense of guilt. Intercourse should be pursued for its own sake and, if the problem is one of anxiety and tension, then a relaxed atmosphere prior to coitus may assist fertilization. Important as a child is, the marital relationship must not be neglected either prior to conception, during pregnancy or after the baby is born.

Nowadays much progress is being achieved to overcome fertility difficulties, but in the euphoria of the biological progress, the interpersonal relationship must not be forgotten.

Abortion

Just as infertility is referred to when there are marital problems, so is termination of pregnancy. Such a termination may have occurred in another relationship or with the husband. When it is mentioned this is an indication that it has left an adverse mark on the psyche. The negative feelings may be associated with persistent guilt feelings and regret that it occurred at all. It may be associated with a poor self-esteem in which the woman is saying that a person who behaves like this is not worthy of love. For other women religious guilt may remain, and the present marital difficulties be explained as a result of God's punishment. Indeed, punishment may be felt to be justified and so prolonged.

But often, when mentioned, abortion is explained on the grounds that the husband or future husband insisted on a termination against the wife's wishes. The consent to the termination is now seen as an act of weakness against a persuasive and dominant man, who did not care about her feelings. The abortion may have generated anger and resentment which still persist, and often the account is portrayed in such a way as to indicate the unpleasant nature of the man who was callous enough to insist on the termination. Now there is anger, guilt and regret that consent was given to such an action. These feelings may surface at a time when the wife is experiencing a depressive period, and the intensity of her feelings should be assessed in the light of her mood.

But generally such a woman wishes to state that her present marital predicament makes sense because it goes back a long way, to the point when she was obliged to have a termination against her will. When the husband is questioned he may admit that he panicked, but on other occasions he is surprised at the criticism because in his recollection the wife consented freely. This is a very good example of how men and women may on the surface consent out of fear and anxiety to acts which they resent, yet later on attack their partner for the same deed now seen in terms of the underlying resentment which prevailed at the time but was not recognized.

Pregnancy

The impact of pregnancy on the marriage has already been noted in that earlier research has found an association between premarital or early marital pregnancy and divorce. American workers have suggested that premarital pregnancy is part of a "divorce-producing syndrome" (Christensen & Rubinstein, 1956). In Britain the findings of Thornes & Collard (1979) confirm the association between the two. There are differences, however, between couples who have had premarital pregnancy but remained married, and those who divorced. The authors, who investigated the divorced and continuously married in detail, state: "In particular the marital relationship of the continuously married with premarital pregnancy appears relative to the divorced, both to have developed from a sounder base and to have begun in an atmosphere more helpful for marital adjustments." For example, the divorced with premarital pregnancy had far shorter courtships than those continuously married, much greater family opposition and much more serious premarital problems with their spouse. Two other findings of these works were that the divorced premarital pregnant came from larger families than the continuously married, and they had the longest duration of post puerperal depression. This study is of the greatest importance in showing that, although premarital pregnancy is associated with divorce (Gibson,

1974; Monahan, 1960; Coombs & Zumeta, 1970) there are additional complications in the divorced. One author found that another connecting link between premarital pregnancy and divorce is the weak financial position of the father (Furstenberg, 1976).

Whatever the origin of pregnancy, it is usually a happy event. But in some women – and particularly in the young and unmarried – it may be a source of stress. In particular a woman needs the support of the father of the baby and, when this is absent, she may have to face a series of problems which are neatly described by one author (Snaith, 1983): "For a young woman in an unstable relationship with her partner the first pregnancy presents an enormous challenge. She may be faced with ambivalent or irresponsible attitudes of the partner, angry or condemnatory postures of the parents and the shallow sympathy of her friends; there may be looming problems of accommodation and reduction of income and the need to give up former entertainments and pursuits. She may be poorly endowed with the personality characteristics necessary for good motherhood and she may have a fear of hospitals, injections and pain. She may feel lonely and react badly to the physical consequences of pregnancy, especially exhaustion, nausea and sickness. As pregnancy progresses she may have problems with weight gain and preoccupation with loss of sexual attractiveness. As she approaches the time of delivery, she may be regaled with harrowing stories of what may go wrong and she may have fears that the child will be deformed or handicapped, especially if instances of this have occurred within her family or among her close acquaintances."

Given all these possibilities which confront many women, the number of women who become psychiatrically ill is small. In a study of 128 pregnant women randomly collected, 17 of them (or 13 per cent) became ill during the whole pregnancy. Most of these cases suffered from affective disorders of anxiety and depression which disappeared post puerperally. A few women remained affected for as long as twelve months after the birth of the baby, and join the post puerperal depressions (Watson et al, 1984).

Illness during pregnancy means that the sexual relationship suffers and so does the interaction of the couple. This dilutes the intimacy of the couple and does not prepare them for the efforts required when the baby arrives. The husband feels rejected and the wife overwhelmed. The husband may find sexual abstention difficult during pregnancy, whether the wife is ill or not. He may have extramarital intercourse or an affair (Curtis, 1955; Lacousciere, 1972). If this is found out later on, the wife feels angry, bitter and resentful, an emotional response which may continue and have an adverse impact on the marriage.

The overwhelming majority of pregnancies result in a normal, healthy baby. A small number end in a neo-natal death. The mother of a stillborn baby feels bewildered and sad, and this may develop into chronic depression, hypochondriasis, phobias or other disturbances (Cullberg J., 1972). Such a reaction may overwhelm the husband, and sexual relations may cease, with all the dangers of losing the man-woman encounter, and gradually he will be responding to the wife as to a deprived friend. The other children of the family may feel guilty in surviving and they may carry problems in the next generation.

The important issue in perinatal death is that the parents should be helped to mourn their baby. They should be encouraged to see and hold the dead baby, keep photographs, register a proper name, attend a funeral and see that a proper grave is marked (Bourne & Lewis, 1984). It is particularly important that mourning be completed before the next pregnancy is undertaken. Such a pregnancy may be difficult, and post puerperal reaction frequent and severe. The next baby may also be at risk if its identity is permanently confused with that of the dead child. Hence, pregnancy should be postponed until mourning has been completed and the marital relationship reasserted.

If the dead baby is not normal and the reality of its death faced, parents may be saddled with persistent bewilderment, uncertainty, anger and self-reproach. All these consume the energy that should be channelled towards the interpersonal relationship of the spouses. When such feelings persist, they place the marriage in peril.

Post Puerperal Syndromes

After the birth of the baby, the mother is subject to a variety of syndromes which are crucial to her health and the welfare of the marriage. In taking a history of marital difficulties of some standing, one of the commonest remarks which is made spontaneously is: "It all started with the birth of Charles/ Jenny/Peter . . . and it has been going on ever since." There is little doubt that if all post puerperal disorders were diagnosed in time, and both treated and counselled, marital breakdown would become less frequent. Hence the importance attached to these conditions in this book. They were pointed out in a publication which came out in 1968 (Dominian) and the passage of time has not lessened their importance. There are three forms of post puerperal syndromes, namely maternal blues, neurotic depression and psychotic illness. Each will be considered in turn, but they have been the subject of many psychiatric publications, listed in a paper by Watson et al. (1984). In general post puerperal syndromes are depressive in nature. Their cause has been widely discussed. Pitt (1968) calls the disorder "atypical depression" and considers it the response to "non-specific stress". In contrast Dalton (1980) believes it is caused by a sharp drop in circulating progesterone in the puerperium.

Maternal Blues

The majority of women who have a baby go through a period of sadness which commences suddenly between the third and tenth day (Stein, 1982). The symptoms include tearfulness, sadness, elation, irritability and negative feelings for the baby and/or the husband. "Maternal blues" usually clear up within days. It is a common state and affects between 60 and 80 per cent (Pitt, 1968; Robins, 1962; Breen, 1975). There is evidence that in a small proportion of women it does not clear up and these then join the more persistent post puerperal depression (Cox et al., 1982).

Neurotic Depression

A depressive picture consisting of tearfulness, despondency, tiredness, lack of sexual feelings, feelings of inadequacy and inability to cope are the characteristics of this affective state, which is clearly distinguished from maternal blues in starting later, some weeks after the birth of the baby, and also being more persistent and severe. The incidence of this condition has been estimated at 3 per cent (Todd, 1964), 16 per cent (Watson et al., 1984) and 14 per cent (Kumar & Robson, 1978). In one of the most detailed studies (Watson et al., 1984), the 16 per cent of post puerperal psychiatric illness was found in the sixth postnatal week, but this figure increased to 22 per cent by the end of the first year after birth. Thus it can be seen that this is an extremely common condition.

Affective disorder of this kind is significantly associated

with a previous psychiatric history, feelings of emotional lability during pregnancy, anxiety, anger and tension and, most important of all from the point of view of this book, the presence of stress and dissatisfaction in the marital relationship. Like maternal blues, post puerperal depression usually clears up within a few months, but not in all cases. In a few it persists for years and, if one is alert to the possibility, one sees women who show chronic tiredness, apathy, loss of sexual desire, irritability, sleep disturbance, changes in weight (gain or loss) many years after the birth of the child. What percentage of these conditions do not clear up completely but enter into a chronic state has not been assessed, but those who do suffer in this way can cause inestimable damage to their marriage.

When these women are examined in more detail certain distinctions are found. The study of Watson et al. (1984) placed them in five groups. In group one there were six women with single episodes of depression unrelated to pregnancy and childbirth. They suffered from bereavement, unexpected redundancy, marital crisis and housing crisis. In group two there were ten cases who became depressed in association with life events related to pregnancy or childbirth, which included premature birth and antenatal complications. In group three there were six women who had continuous life difficulties including marital difficulties. In group four there were four women all of whom had experienced bereavement during the pregnancy or in previous pregnancies. In group five there were three women who became depressed with no obvious precipitating factor.

Thus it can be seen that post puerperal depression has a heterogeneous group of precipitating causes, all of which should be considered during the pregnancy, so that a certain degree of anticipated counselling can be introduced.

Psychotic Illness

As against neurotic depression, which is a comparatively common condition, a post puerperal psychotic illness is rare and is of the order of one in five hundred births (Granville-Grossman, 1971). The symptoms are emotional lability, anxiety, distractability, pressurized speech, insomnia, depression, perplexity, agitation, auditory and visual hallucinations, delusions, apathy and hypomania. This is a spectrum of affective, schizophrenic and organic features (Sneddon & Kerry, 1980). This condition is now called schizo-affective and is an acute mental illness which needs hospitalization; depending on the clinical picture, a mother and baby unit is one place for such a mother. It has been found that 94 per cent of puerperal psychoses had an onset within four weeks and 65 per cent within two weeks of birth (Protheroe, 1969). These conditions need treatment with appropriate medication or E.C.T. The prognosis is very good and they rarely play a contribution to marital breakdown.

Post Puerperal Depression and Marriage

From the available research evidence it is clear that a small number of maternal blues join the much larger number of neurotic depression, and that a proportion of these conditions may last for a long time – months or even years (Brown & Harris, 1978; Frommer & O'Shea, 1973). They are, as already stated, characterized by persistent symptoms of depression, loss of pleasure, ease of tiredness, fatigue, irritability, insomnia, weight changes and – above all – sexual indifference, with sometimes aggression towards the husband. These women become withdrawn, sink into a state of apathy and neglect themselves. They do not want to go out with their husband, cease to entertain, rarely visit friends except the immediate family and channel all their energy into survival. They have difficulty in looking after the baby and the house, or they become obsessionally tidy but have no time for anything else. They refuse sexual intercourse and indeed may not want to be touched at all. In some instances they show a constant irritation towards their husband, who has done nothing to deserve it.

The husband initially makes allowances and puts it all down to the baby: the mother is often awakened at night and, in any case, the baby tires her. For some months he will assist to the best of his ability and accept sexual abstinence. Gradually, however, it will dawn on him that time is passing and there is no change. Patience will slowly turn to irritability and anger. Instead of kindness he will blame his wife for her behaviour. Words like "lazy", "slut" and "selfish" will fly around. He will now take a moral stand and slowly turn accusatory: "What she needs is to be shaken out of her laziness." "A kick in the backside is what she needs." He may force himself on her sexually and she may agree reluctantly to his demands, without any basic change to her feelings.

Another version of this deterioration in the marital relationship is the case when marital difficulties existed prior to the post puerperal depression. In this instance all that will happen is that the already bad situation will become worse.

If the condition is not diagnosed the marriage will gradually deteriorate. An apathy will descend on the couple, who will hardly relate to each other in any way. They will cease doing anything together, talking to each other or having sex, and the marriage will become a ghost relationship, or there will be constant arguments over sex, with episodes of violence.

Sometimes the picture is not clear and all that is seen is a prevailing mood of irritability and misery which does not lift. The relationship with the husband and children is poor and, if the post puerperal syndrome is not identified, blame will be laid on the poor marital situation which is interpreted as causing the trouble, instead of recognizing that the marital difficulties are the aftermath of the post puerperal depression.

This is a picture which any health visitor, nurse, social worker or doctor should recognize and for which they should initiate treatment. The treatment may consist of anti-depressants, but even more importantly, the couple should have the condition explained to them. This will lift an enormous amount of self-criticism and guilt on the part of the wife, who is utterly perplexed by her state. The husband's support and availability need to be mobilized. Advice should be offered on the practical side of running the home and looking after the baby in such a way that the mother can have time and rest for herself. If necessary and possible, help should be obtained. The relatives should also be informed so that they can provide extra support. It is important that no further pregnancy should be undertaken – the author has seen such clinically depressed women plunge into new pregnancies, producing a situation in which the mother cannot cope at all.

If post puerperal depression is kept in mind, particularly by the health visitor, then an eminently treatable condition can be identified in time, before it causes utter havoc to the marriage (Wrate et al., 1985).

6. Marital Satisfaction in the Early Years

NEWARK COMMUNITY MENTAL HEALTH TEAM
SOCIAL SERVICES
RECEIVED
MAR 1989

Marital Satisfaction

The first five years of marriage have been shown to be crucial, in that there is a high rate of marital breakdown and that the marital experience during these early years influences the outcome of marriage later on. One obvious link between these early years and marriage is the level of marital satisfaction. Up to twenty years ago there was little understanding of marital satisfaction, complex as the concept is. Then, using the idea of the family cycle – that is, dividing marriage into stages before the children's arrival, pre-school, primary school, secondary school, launching of the children and the empty nest – marital satisfaction was examined throughout the cycle. According to a crucial paper by Rollings & Canon (1974), there was a general decline in satisfaction in the early stages but an increase in the later ones when the children are leaving home and the stage of the empty nest is reached. A British study (Walker, 1977) has found similar results. This study analysed several components of satisfaction and found that the standard of living does not suffer much, but there is a continuous dissatisfaction with the way finances are handled. Companionship and understanding in marriage decline from the beginning and do not rise until the children are in secondary school. The parameters which show the worst decline are the expression of love and the sexual side of the relationship. This particular finding is of immense importance in the light of the movement of contemporary marriage towards an intimate relationship of love and affection. In fact, this same study finds that British wives are least satisfied with the expression of affection, that more companionship and understanding is expected, although they are more satisfied with the material aspects of marriage. A preliminary analysis of the British findings suggests that within the overall pattern there are sub groups. The lower socio-economic group showed lower levels of satisfaction throughout, compared with the higher socio-economic group. Those married under twenty showed earlier decline than those who married later.

Other work in Britain confirms the general decline of marital satisfaction. A study of working-class women with children at home found that four in ten of the women experienced considerable dissatisfaction with their marriage or little joy from it (Brown & Harris, 1978). Another study, also in Britain, found that 73 per cent of the sample of mothers with five-month-old babies reported a decline in marital happiness (Oakley, 1979).

How are we to account for this drop in marital satisfaction from the beginning of marriage? Research is scant and what follows is based on a mixture of clinical observation before the advent of children and the more extensive research evidence after their arrival.

Idealization

The process of courtship is being examined at the Marriage Research Centre and its results will appear in a forthcoming publication (Mansfield, 1986). The same research writer has commented on the topic before (Mansfield, 1982). What is psychologically indisputable is that during the later phases of courtship idealization exists.

Idealization is a psychological process whereby the loved

one is seen in the best possible light. Their good points are exaggerated and their faults minimized and excused. Every effort is made to see the other as untouched by human frailty. This affirmative feeling is responded to by behaving in the best possible way.

But there are other elements of courtship which stand out. The first is that of the time spent together. Far more time is spent together than probably at any other time during the subsequent relationship. This proximity means that the young couple return to the closeness and intimacy of the parent/young child relationship. There is a feeling of total belonging to one another, with an exclusiveness that is deeply appreciated. In this closeness there is an intensity of affection expressed with words, action and touch. The couple are likely to find themselves in each other's arms more often than at any time thereafter.

This closeness is associated with a desire to please. Birthdays and special occasions are remembered, presents and treats are exchanged and shared. There is a powerful affirmative emphasis on the ego of the other person, who exists in a significant manner.

Quarrels take place but are not frequent or destructive. There is little risk of persistent criticism, deflating remarks and/or humiliating experiences, in whose presence the courtship is unlikely to continue. Reconciliation is often swift and there is a readiness to admit joint responsibility for what has gone wrong, instead of blaming one another.

Thus courtship is a positive experience, which is usually described as "falling in love". The childhood characteristics of feeling recognized, wanted and appreciated are experienced to the full. Both partners are on their best behaviour in order to impress each other.

After the wedding there is no longer any need to impress. The traditional wedding vows refer to the commitment for "better or worse". The hunt is over and the prey has been safely landed. Nobody doubts that there is a relaxation of effort, and inevitably there is a reduction of communication, companionship and intimacy, together with a rise of disappointments, unpleasant surprises, quarrels and frustrations. During courtship the couple talked endlessly into the early hours of the morning. After the marriage the husband reads his paper or watches television. Before, a lot of time was spent together. Afterwards he returns to the pub, club or male friends, and she visits the family.

Before, a lot of the time spent together would be hand in hand or in each other's arms. Afterwards physical intimacy declines. Appearances, which were at their very best before, now change as the wife is not always dressed up. Unpleasant personal habits appear. Husbands are found to be bad at dealing with correspondence, money and other male role responsibilities. The wife's poor cooking emerges as her limited repertoire is soon exhausted. The missing clean shirt syndrome may rear its ugly head. And finally there is the perennial problem of personal hygiene. Women often complain that men don't wash often enough, and in the author's experience this is a complaint which is almost exclusively made by the wife.

Far more serious is the increase of arguments and quarrels. These are no longer reasonable exchanges, and the destructiveness of blaming each other instead of assuming joint responsibility creeps in. All these reductions in satisfaction gradually lead to a minority of couples complaining, and one or other partner will begin to feel and think: "This is not the man or woman I married. He or she has changed." And this minority, in whom respect for spouse dwindles, will either proceed to immediate departure or at least feel that they have made a serious mistake. They will now continue in the marriage with a growing uncertainty as to whether they wish to stay in it or not. When other adverse events follow, they will supervene on an already exhausted spouse, who will not need much stress before deciding to go.

But, of course, it is only a small number of marriages that let their disappointment shake the basic commitment to the union. The majority will adapt, and change from falling in love to loving. In loving, the expectations will change from idealization to reality. They will continue to love the same person but now accept that there are limitations to communication, affection, intimacy and sexuality. What is missed in frequency and quantity will be compensated for by quality.

Communication will continue and the spouses will discover the deeper layers of each other. They will become acquainted with the wounds which each will bring to the marriage from their childhood, and this knowledge will enhance their concern for one another and lead to a chance of healing. This healing will occur as the partners give each other another opportunity for recognition and acceptance (Dominian, 1981). Crises of illness, bereavement or unemployment will bring out of the partners qualities of care, sympathy and forbearance which will deepen their bonds. The emergence of minor (and sometimes troublesome) complaints of occasional headaches, migraine, mood swings, premenstrual tension, anxiety or fears will allow the partners to show a tolerance and understanding hitherto unexperienced.

The intensity of affection may recede. Couples may not reiterate feelings of "I love you" every time they see each other. In fact they will take for granted that they are loved by all the daily events of life. The time spent together in conversation, in social activity, doing things jointly, tackling the house or sharing finances will all contribute to the sense of mutual concern. The moments of overt expression of affection will mean that much more simply because of the surprise element in them.

The frequency of sexual intercourse will vary, but during the first year of marriage, as the couple learn to adjust to each other sexually, intercourse becomes a powerful verification of the mutual significance they have for each other. It will be a united effort to discover what pleases, and in doing so they will plumb the depths of one another.

In loving there is a whole series of unlearning and new learning to be done. Each partner enters marriage with the heightened perception of courtship. (Today's increasingly common period of cohabitation will have to be studied carefully to find out whether it is a period of prolonged courtship or part of the marriage experience.) Some of these perceptions will be confirmed but modified. "Yes, he is on the whole patient, understanding, caring but he does get mad if I keep him waiting; he does not like to be bothered by small details and he does get infuriated if I am too childish and he is jealous." "Yes, she is patient, understanding and caring but she also loses her temper out of the blue, cannot understand my logic and gets furious if I am late for meals. And who would have thought that this gorgeous creature would insist on making love with the lights out, will not undress in front of me, will lock the bathroom door, can't stand being tickled, and really enjoys sex only when half sozzled?"

Loving is an expression of the continuing desire to be with the chosen person. It is an unconditional commitment to a person not a dream. The intensity of affectivity gives way to the security and trust of the availability of the spouse, who will not abandon us however horrible we are temporarily, however unattractive we may be in our bodies, minds and feelings for a duration of time. Marital love expresses the same certainty as the child experiences in the presence of loving parents who nurture, facilitate and affirm. In terms of marital love the author has stated that its characteristics are the sustaining, healing and growth promoting of the couple (Dominian, 1981).

The Impact of the Child on Marriage Satisfaction

If the dissolution of idealization is one of the challenges of the shift from being in love to loving, then the shift from the couple into a family of three is the other. In his interesting study Clulow (1982) quotes various remarks made by parents on the arrival of the first baby:

"I can honestly say that for the first six months the baby put a tremendous strain on both my husband and myself as individuals, and our marriage as well."

"We have given up the freedom to choose where we go and when we go, as consideration must be given to meal times and whether a baby, pram, etc. is acceptable. Each outing is a major expedition and not just a question of up and away. This can be a strain in the relationship as before you had only each other to consider."

"Six weeks after the birth my husband and I had intercourse. I was quite frightened that the stitches would not take. I know my husband was also frightened about hurting me. Now the fears have ceased."

And perhaps the most telling of all is the following statement:

"Babies do not recognize Sundays as being different from any other day."

In fact there are two schools of thought. One considers that the first birth is traumatic and the other that it is a fulfilling experience.

In American studies one author favours the crisis concept (Le Masters, 1957). Tiredness, social isolation, a drop in housekeeping standards, the feeling of being unkempt were all worries of the wife, and the husband added the concern of extra financial responsibility and reduced sexual interest of the wife. This temporary deterioration of sexual intercourse after birth has been noted by many workers (Hamilton, 1962; Frommer & O'Shea, 1973; Udenberg, 1974; Oakley, 1979). Clearly the reaction of the mother to her baby is crucial in terms of the confirmation of her identity and role as a woman, and therefore of her self-esteem, which in turn safeguards her marital and sexual relationship.

In the previous chapter reference was made to post puerperal depression. This clearly has a most intrusive impact on both marriage and sex life. Physical factors such as reduction of progesterone have been offered as explanations, but what of alternative explanations?

In Britain, Brown & Harris (1978) and Oakley (1979 and 1980) have offered social reasons. Brown & Harris related postnatal depression to life events, but only in conjunction with a poor marriage, housing, employment and finance. Thus working-class women were more prone to depression, as well as all women who had three or more children under the age of fourteen at home, who had lost their own mother under the age of eleven and who had no intimate male support. Oakley relates the depression to high technology, in particular "maternal blues" to instrumental deliveries and epidural analgesia. For Oakley social factors and medical management are the crucial factors responsible for the high incidence of depression.

Brown & Harris's observation of the predisposing factor of loss of a mother before the age of eleven is related to a psychodynamic explanation of motherhood, namely that it is the relationship with her mother that makes a woman handle motherhood well. If she has had a good and satisfying relationship with her mother, she has internalized the notion of motherhood which is freshly expressed in herself, with no conflict or trauma. If a good mother was missing, then the likelihood of distress is more common (Frommer & O'Shea, 1973; Breen, 1975).

Thus it can be seen that the impact of a child on marriage will have serious implications, particularly when the mother is depressed because she is likely to withdraw from her husband emotionally and sexually. But even when she is not depressed, there is a reduction of the time which is available to her husband, an increase in fatigue (Walker, 1969) and with this some reduction in sexual activity.

The child itself, particularly when it becomes a little older, may become a source of conflict for the parents. The mother may take the child into bed with her against the protestation of the husband, who feels pushed out and inhibited in sexual activity. Another complaint – this time offered by wives – is that husbands become besotted with their child and will spoil it with attention. Wives find such behaviour difficult, as they may feel displaced or ignored. The husband may come home and, after a perfunctory greeting to his wife, will direct his attention entirely to the child. On the other hand, the husband may ignore the baby and his wife, and pursue his leisure as before, leaving the wife a prisoner at home. Finally, the parents may begin to disagree on how to bring up the child. The usual conflict is to be found with the mother who wants to adopt a flexible and lenient attitude, and the father who wishes to treat the young child as a grown-up and to impose a strict discipline. Whatever the source of conflict, if it is persistent and irreconcilable, it drives a serious wedge into the relationship of the couple.

The second view of childbirth is that it is a good experience (Hobbs & Cole, 1976). When this happens the baby becomes truly an extension of the love of the couple. Its care becomes a dual responsibility, intimacy is maintained and so is sexual life. The growth of the child becomes a shared achievement, and the undoubted difficulties are seen as transient normal challenges to marriage.

7. The Middle and Late Years

Introduction

Attention has been drawn to the crucial importance of the first five years of marriage, when a third of all marital breakdown occurs, and to the fact that the interpersonal atmosphere established between the spouses has an enduring impact on the rest of the marriage. If the couple marry at the mean age of 25.7 for men and 23.4 for women (*Population Trends*, 1985) then these couples will have reached the age of thirty or near it after completing five years of marriage. In the schema which the author has proposed, there are two other stages, namely the phase between thirty and fifty, defined by the menopause and the launching of the children, and between fifty and the death of one spouse (Dominian, 1980). In this chapter the two phases have been amalgamated.

During the middle years the couple are responsible for the growth of their children, respond to their own development as persons (Lidz, 1976), negotiate crises such as the illness and death of parents, illness in the family, work and unemployment, and emotional development. It is a phase marked by change and increasing awareness of self and spouse.

The later years see a return to a one-to-one relationship. The children have now gone and the parents are entering into new relationships with sons- and daughters-in-law and the grandchildren. The possibility of reproduction is over, and a new meaning of intimacy enters sexuality. These are the years of early or late retirement, an evaluation of what has been achieved, and the exploration of new interests. The departure of children allows couples who have felt dissatisfied with their marriage and delayed leaving until the children grew up, to depart. These divorces late in the life of the couples are surprising to outsiders, but are often friendly and amicable for the couple who have gradually drifted apart. This is not always the case and sometimes one partner is staggered by the decision of their spouse to go. They had no idea that their partner had any such intention, and the departure initiates a profound mourning process not easily alleviated.

The changes will be considered, as for the early years, in terms of social, emotional, intellectual and spiritual dimensions. The sexual one will be treated separately in Chapter 8.

Social

The social changes during the middle years involve success or failure at work and the financial consequences, adverse health of the couple, the growth of their children, and the health of their parents. These factors will be considered in turn.

The core of social change during these years manifests itself in the work situation, most frequently of the husband and less often of the wife. Success will be coupled with financial advance, change of house and a new style of living. Change of house is on the whole welcomed by both spouses, but rarely there is one spouse – normally the wife – who finds the change threatening. She can be removed from her surroundings, her relatives and friends, leaving the North for example, and moving to the South. This loss of the extended network can be very disturbing. It is often accompanied by a more demanding job for the husband, who spends less time at home, and the combination of isolation and loneliness can make a woman feel depressed. In turn she will need to depend more on her husband, and if he is not available the result is increased family stress. Other stress-related situations associated with work can emerge when the husband has to go overseas alone or is frequently absent abroad on business. If the wife is not supported by an effective social network, or leads an emotional life which is markedly dependent on her husband, then his absences are experienced as frequent losses which sometimes she cannot bear. If her complaints are not heeded, such a wife may develop various psychosomatic symptoms and become ill. Illness may force the husband to change his work. Another complaint of wives is that their husbands leave them for long periods and neither write nor ring. They feel forgotten and abandoned, and they hate the absences. Finally promotion may bring extra work, which is undertaken in the evenings and at weekends thus reducing the available intimacy, which may distress the wife making her feel neglected.

Another feature of success is experienced in the new circle of friends acquired by the husband. He relates to new people and wants his wife to share the new experiences. Often this is negotiated without difficulty, but occasionally it can become a problem. The wife may find the new friends unacceptable. Their values and outlook may clash with hers. In particular this applies to women who have worked hard to promote the academic or business future of their husbands. They have made many sacrifices on his behalf which are at first deeply appreciated, but as the husband succeeds and enters an admiring world of friends, he may forget his wife and her contribution. In fact he may wish to forget his humble origins altogether and with this the constant reminder of his beginnings – his wife. She reminds him of the past and he sees her as an impediment to a new life. Such a woman is rejected, and naturally feels very bitter at the way she is treated.

Nowadays women can increasingly be equally successful. They may acquire highly paid jobs, be recognized at work and be entertained during the day in their own right, returning at night to a situation where the husband reasserts his superiority. He may envy her success and her salary, and translate his envy into hostility and humiliation. He may become irritable, blame her for everything that goes wrong at home and with the children, explaining it on the grounds of her absence from home.

The middle years are not always associated with success. Husbands may become unemployed, sick, or turn to alcohol, gambling or drugs. In all these circumstances there is a downward social trend with reduced income, loss of self-respect, irritation and angry outbursts. The wife may remain loyal and stay, or find the atmosphere intolerable and depart.

These are the years when generally the couple remain healthy, but there are exceptions. Physical illness may strike, e.g. neoplasm of the breast and depression is not uncommon in women in their forties. Illness of any duration is a crucial test for spouses. During it anxiety rises, the sick person becomes much more emotionally needy, the healthy one has to take on the duties of both and has to show extra care and solicitude. Most wives are capable of managing the husband's illness; husbands are not so good. Women often complain that their husbands hate them being ill, sometimes to the point of doubting the validity of their illness, particularly if it is psychological in nature: "Are you sure you aren't imagining it?" is a not uncommon question when wives complain of headaches, tiredness, backache, or loss of enjoyment. Often these women are suffering from a covert depressive illness, and their husbands' attitude seems callous, unconcerned and rejecting. They know they are unwell and have to drag themselves around feeling half-dead, yet still being expected to complete all their duties. Such behaviour from the husband erodes the sense of being cared for. It is often noted by wives that when their husbands are ill the whole world needs to know, but when a wife is indisposed the main concern of the husband is the speed of her recovery. Sometimes either spouse finds illness repellent and simply cannot carry out any nursing duties. A feature which appears from time to time clinically is the opposite pattern in which a husband devotes himself to the needs of his chronically ill wife, abstaining from sex for the whole duration of her incapacity only to discover that when she recovers he cannot approach her sexually.

Occasionally parents have to deal with chronic illness in their children, for instance asthma, epilepsy or more serious ones such as fibrocystic disease, crippling neurological disorders or mental handicap. Such conditions in the children may either act as a challenge and unite the couple, or one spouse may be filled with persistent guilt, anxiety, over-concern or an excessive preoccupation with the child to the detriment of the other spouse, or translate it into an enduring negative reaction to sexual intercourse. Usually it is the mother who is so enmeshed with the child, but sometimes the father reacts in this way and takes over. Such a man insists on doing everything for the child, seeks repeated medical advice which is either regarded as not satisfactory or carried out to the letter of the law. The other children feel neglected and so does the wife. The marriage suffers enormously and may not survive. The engagement of one parent to the exclusion of the other plays a prominent part in such family disorders. The failure of one spouse to support the other is also present in typical adolescent problems, in particular premarital sex, cohabitation, pregnancy, smoking, drugs or alcohol.

The spouses' own parents begin to become increasingly incapacitated during these middle years. When a parent becomes ill, particularly if the illness is prolonged, this creates a great deal of stress, often in the wife, who has to support both sets of parents, her own and those of her husband. Sometimes the demands are resented and the suppressed anger is vented against the husband. Often the process of looking after the ailing parent is extremely demanding and may erode the available time of the spouses, who become irritable with each other. After the death of one parent, the other may have to be taken care of in the matrimonial home and such an invasion, if not agreed as a common policy, may be a source of continuous conflict between the spouses.

These stressful events do not often lead by themselves to marital breakdown. What they can do is to add additional stress to the disappointments of the early years, test crucially the quality of care of the spouses and, if trust has already been eroded for other reasons, then these social events finalize the disenchantment or may precipitate the crisis which makes the couple seek help.

During the late years the couple are affected by the departure of their children, the empty-nest stage. Some parents have lived only through their children and when they depart there is not only a deep sense of loss but the couple look at each other and see a stranger. It often happens that each partner has derived their meaning from the relationship with their children. They have lived, eaten and made love with each other but the important significant element of the marriage has been the children. So when they go there is little left to the relationship. This has been particularly true of earlier cohorts of marriage, which emphasized exclusively the importance of marriage in terms of family rather than as an interpersonal relationship. But as already indicated, some couples have become disenchanted with the marriage long before the children depart and have simply awaited that departure before they too leave.

Emotional

Emotional change is very frequently a cause of marital breakdown. In the early years of marriage there is a quick and sudden awareness that one partner is unacceptable because he or she no longer fits in with the expectations of the other. But during the middle years the awareness of incompatibility is slower and arises from the growth of the personality of one spouse. The concept of growth is a dynamic one. The usual assumption is that at the time of marriage one or both partners were immature, that is to say, they had not reached a stage of assuming enough autonomy to run their own lives, were still desirous of direction and control from an authority figure, lacked a sense of internal direction and confidence, became easily anxious and needed external support, and lacked sufficient self-esteem to a degree where they accepted blame and criticism for something going wrong when clearly it was not their fault. The sort of childhood that such a person had fills the pages of many textbooks. A combination of inheritance and various unsatisfactory upbringing patterns produces such a person, who may flee from home as a means of gaining independence and marry early before twenty. But emotional immaturity may persist to later ages.

A number of events begin to change the personality of such an emotionally dependent person. Study and work may show the individual that they are not inept, giving them intellectual confidence. The negotiation of repeated small crises of physical pain, emotional disappointment, hurt rejection and criticism gradually endows the spouse with the sense of containing distress without rushing to the partner for comfort. Pregnancy and childrearing give the woman a sense of achievement and the feeling that she is as good as her mother. Achievement may impinge on either spouse other than through study and work. Looking after the house, shopping, handling money, discussion with the spouse, relatives and friends, and finding that one is right in one's opinions and intuitions give a sense of trust in oneself. The handling of periods of being alone, unsupported and bereaved gives a feeling of coping with isolation. Dynamic psychology would interpret the changes in terms of a reduction of fantasies, and behaviourism will explain the maturation as a result of unlearning patterns of fear and incompetence, learning skills and acquiring confidence. Whatever the explanation – and in practice it is a combination of both – the end result is a change in the image of oneself. There is a strengthened sense of one's identity as a person separate from parents and spouse. This is realized in a much greater feeling of autonomy, the ability to survive on one's own, to take the initiative and handle difficulties. There is a deepening of self-esteem. The person no longer feels inept and lacking goodness; rather, that he deserves care, attention and love. There is also a decrease in the sense of guilt and an increase in the ability to face life with hope and optimism.

This change from dependence to independence is a transformation that takes place in the majority of human beings. It is a gradual process which begins in the teens and twenties, gathers momentum in the thirties, and can continue into the forties and fifties. It is a process that has a profound impact on marriage and is often the single most important pathology of the middle and late years of marriage (Dominian, 1968).

In the thirties and forties it can be seen in either spouse, but it is particularly evident in wives. The story may be of a woman who marries early in her life. She often chooses a dominant, strong, extrovert person who is seen as a continuation of a parental figure. This figure may be idealized, or there may be ambivalent attitudes towards him;

that is to say, a conscious acceptance of his authority and an unconscious hostility carried over from attitudes to parents. This hostility emerges later on and the once-loved figure becomes someone who is frequently criticized.

Assuming that the husband is accepted unconditionally, then the wife is prepared to be directed, told what to do, given advice, her clothes bought for her, the money handled by him, the holidays arranged for her, the car driven by him, the house chosen largely on his advice, his friends becoming her friends, his ideas hers, and in general he runs her life for her. For some years this arrangement may work well. They are seen as a happy couple. He shows her off, and she respects and admires him.

Imperceptibly things change. As a result of the reasons given above, the wife will slowly begin to develop. At the start she may simply ask to drive the car or have a say in the decisions affecting the children or the holidays. In normal marriages this increased involvement will be welcomed. But in the marriages that run into difficulty, every request for change will be blocked. The husband will say that driving is dangerous, that she should not bother her head about money, he will look after all that and, as far as the children are concerned, surely she does not expect him to give them a worse education than he had himself, so they will go to the school he determines.

For a while the wife may accept the refusal to take her seriously. But this is a temporary cessation of her independence. She will reiterate the same and additional requests. The requests will become more imperative and sound like demands. Now she *demands* to be taken seriously. If the husband still refuses to respond, then arguments and quarrels begin. These quarrels will escalate in intensity and frequency. The wife feels like a prisoner, and her husband – once her champion – is now experienced as a jailer. She will break ranks and start associating with girl friends who are undergoing similar experiences, or join a feminist movement. Her husband will usually complain bitterly about the bad company she keeps. He will attack her friends, deriding their and her views of autonomy and equality. For good measure he will warn her to watch out, because her friends appear to be divorced and if she is not careful she will go that way. This is usually given as a warning – but little does he know that her thoughts are already veering in that direction.

But she is not yet ready to go. She is still unsure of herself; her children are a deep concern, she is afraid of the aloneness of separation and still has hope that her husband will change. But the hope fades. The arguments become more severe, her anger may spill over and she finds herself withdrawing from sex. Her unavailability sexually may lead her husband to become aggressive and hurt her, turn to alcohol or increasingly spend more time away from home. His refusal to change is often a marked expression of anxiety. He is afraid that if he yields to any of her requests to change there will be no end to possible changes. He is afraid to let go and lose power because he expects the tables to be reversed. He believes that if he is not in control of her then she will control him. In desperation he begins to forbid her to go out, meet her friends or do the things she wants to do. By now her confidence is mounting, her fury increasing and she refuses to comply. Not only is she not available sexually, but in the end she may refuse to cook or look after him. She is out most of the time. This is a tense situation in which the husband may become increasingly agitated, and sometimes casualty departments see the bloodbath that ensues from such fights. At last the wife will leave the home.

Then a strange course of events will take place. One might think that the "strong" man will be able to look after himself, leave his wife alone in her search for independence and look after his children. But this is not the picture that often presents itself clinically. On the contrary, the husband becomes very agitated and, when his wife leaves, starts ringing all her friends frantically. He realizes that he cannot exist without her and is truly very dependent on her. He will drink excessively and make pathetic pleas on his knees for her to come back, promising everything that she wants.

Sometimes this works. Often it does not. The wife has found her strength, her independence, her confidence and simply finds her husband redundant. His pathetic pleas make her recognize that behind his bullying is a child, and she may despise him after this discovery. Or she may in fact return, only to find that after a short while the husband returns to his old ways and further remonstration has no effect on him. Next time she leaves she will do so for good. But sometimes the cycle is repeated several times before she finally goes.

Another variation of this theme is the pattern whereby the husband not only promises to change but actually does so. He puts in an enormous effort to understand, communicate, please and be available. However, now that the husband is ready to comply with her wishes, the wife is no longer able to receive his changed behaviour. She acknowledges that he has changed, but has discovered that she no longer loves him. The years of frustration have taken their toll, and her image of the husband has become negative. There is a general attrition: trust has become exhausted and so has her respect for him. She is friendly, means no harm to him, would like him to find another woman and be happy, but she realizes that she is no longer willing to be his wife. She does not love him, despite his protestations that he loves her. This clinical picture is seen repeatedly by all counsellors and is often a signal that reconciliation will not succeed. The wife sometimes comes for help, not to be reconciled but to show goodwill or to hand over her acutely distressed husband into the counsellor's hands so that she can leave with her conscience clear. This is particularly the case when the husband threatens suicide, which frightens her, and she wants to make sure that he has someone to turn to before she goes. Sometimes the wife is sure that the marriage is over and she wants to go, but she cannot leave her inept husband behind. She comes to counselling for his sake, without any intention of really reconciling herself to him again.

Such a wife who finds her identity, autonomy and self-esteem is likely to make a much more mature choice in a further marriage, as opposed to the marriages that dissolve early on when the couple have not had time to achieve these maturational objectives.

This movement towards independence may extend into the fifties, and here the clinical picture is often that it is the husband who is the late developer. After twenty or more years of marriage he decides to have an affair, go to the other woman and leave his wife. An analysis of such marriages often shows that a sense of duty and loyalty has kept him going for over two decades. Gradually he has come to realize that the choice of his wife was not an independent one, but influenced by parents or the desire to marry. Now he feels sufficiently grown up to marry a woman with whom there is a much greater emphasis on sex and affection than on the duties of the previous marriage. Such divorces are particularly painful to the wife, who often finds her husband's behaviour incomprehensible.

Intermediate between continuation and departure are the patterns of behaviour in which the dependent spouse has affairs to show independence, but never actually intends to leave home. The affairs are symptomatic of the desire to be grown up and, if interpreted correctly, they can lead to a readjustment in the marriage.

Intellectual

Change in cognition also takes place in these middle and late years. The couple may change their views, attitudes, opinions and ideas together, or one of them may develop his or her changes unilaterally. Thus change in outlook can often be integrated into a stable marriage. Political views may change and the spouses vote for different political parties. Attitudes to war and nuclear weapons may vary sharply. Such differences rarely contribute to marital breakdown by themselves. But breakdown is a complex phenomenon of gradual attrition in these years. Whereas differentiation can often be an enrichment, fundamental differences may become the occasions for subtle attacks on each other: "You are a fool, only a fool can really believe in that politician . . . You are naïve to be taken in by their promises."

Intellectual changes may lead to one partner wishing to go to the theatre whilst the other is not interested in drama or music but prefers to watch television. It is clear from all clinical experience and research studies that feelings, emotions and sexuality are far more influential factors in the contribution to breakdown. But when the affective relationship is in balance then the alienation at the intellectual level may lead to the frequent statement: "We have nothing in common: we don't do anything together. He simply works and pokes fun at what he deigns to call my brain."

Spiritual

There are not only intellectual but also spiritual changes in the middle and late years. For couples who initially practised their faith, the cessation of one doing so may be a grievous blow to the other. In denominations where regular attendance at services on Sunday is an essential part of the faith, the non-attendance of one partner may have painful repercussions, particularly when the children are taken by the other spouse. The family is complete during the rest of the week but not on Sunday. The practising member feels deprived of a vital support. The cessation of practice may be accompanied by changes in moral standards and in sexual behaviour, to the consternation of the partner. This alienation is painful but can be coped with. Sometimes, however, the defecting parent attacks the faith of their spouse and even derides it before the children, sowing a good deal of confusion, and causing much pain to the practising partner who is now held in ridicule for their childish beliefs.

With the passage of time there may be a change in values. Couples may frequently quarrel about the type of schooling they wish to give their children, whether they should opt for more material aggrandizement and harder work, or spend more time enjoying each other's company, pursue simplicity or the complexity of urban life – give up the rat race, retire early or even change the style of life altogether. Thus a number of men give up lucrative occupations and join the ministry or some form of social work. Women may suddenly find themselves becoming the vicar's wife, with totally different expectations.

Once again changes in the spiritual life or in values often do not lead to marital breakdown. But when the preceding years have put the marriage into a vulnerable state, then alterations from deeply held beliefs and orientations may be the final straw that breaks the camel's back.

8. The Middle and Late Years — the Sexual Dimension

There are three important characteristics in sexual life in the middle and late years. The first is related to the husband, and is concerned with a reduction of male sexual drive leading to impotence in the later decades. The second is connected with the wife and the menopause. The third is the presence of extramarital relations.

Male Sexual Activity

Sexual intercourse in marriage continues during these years at a mean frequency of about three acts of coitus per week in the thirties, and around twice a week in the forties and fifties (Kinsey et al., 1948). The restrictions are imposed by individual spouses whose sexual drive is limited by physical or psychological reasons. Wives in particular may show a loss of interest after the birth of any child. Unless the relationship deteriorates for personal reasons, sexual difficulties are not common in the thirties and forties. A small percentage of women, which Kinsey found to be of the order of 10 per cent, find it difficult or impossible to obtain an orgasm (Kinsey et al., 1953). The inability to obtain orgasm does not stop a woman from enjoying her sexual life, and anorgasmia by itself is rarely a cause of marital breakdown.

The problem of the man is that of erectile impotence which gradually increases with age. Although impotence can begin in the middle forties, its incidence is still low, under 10 per cent in the middle fifties, and does not rise steeply until the late seventies. Husbands referred for sexual difficulties during the middle and late years have to be clearly differentiated into two categories, namely those who suffer from psychological difficulties and can be helped, and those who are experiencing impotence of a biological nature, which is usually permanent. But all husbands suffering from impotence in the thirties, forties, fifties and even sixties are worth detailed sexual examinations, in case physiological reasons can be identified and corrected.

When the problem is not of impotence but rather loss of sexual desire, care must be taken to distinguish between loss of sexual desire altogether, or only with a particular partner. Sometimes men may appear to be uninterested in their wives when they are perfectly capable of performing sexually with other women.

A biological loss of potency is understood and adapted to by the majority of wives. It is rarely a cause of marital breakdown, but the wife must be helped to appreciate the nature of the problem, otherwise she may feel that her husband must be having sex with someone else. When she appreciates that this is not the case, but that a genuine problem exists, she can learn to live with it.

Sometimes impotence may be caused by physical factors, of which neurological disorders and diabetes are common.

Menopause

The menopause has been recognized for thousands of years. It is characterized by the cessation of menstruation and it occurs usually at the age of fifty-one. It is accompanied by hot flushes and sweating, and less frequently by insomnia, palpitations, dizziness, anxiety and depression, and physically there is a long-term accompaniment of osteoporosis and cardiovascular involvement. Although 70 to 80 per cent of women experience flushes and sweats, only about 20 per cent consult their doctor, and about 10 per cent will require treatment.

Marital Breakdown and the Menopause

Statistics show that there are two peaks of divorce. The first is in the first five to nine years of marriage. The second, which is smaller, is after twenty or more years of marriage (*Social Trends*, 1976). This second rise is a complex phenomenon often associated with long-standing difficulties which have not been resolved, the couple having waited for the departure of the children before separating.

But are there any specific upheavals of the menopause itself which may contribute to marital breakdown? The specific upheavals are threefold: social factors, psychological illness and psychological problems.

Social

At about the time of the menopause, three events impinge on the marriage. These have been mentioned before and are briefly recapitulated here. The children are going through adolescence and there are many anxieties about young people behaving promiscuously, living together, becoming pregnant, turning to drugs or alcohol. The marital problem is often associated with the fact that the father has been a distant figure, and the mother has had the major share of the upbringing of the children. When adolescence arrives, the associated problems become too much for her and she calls on the assistance of the father, who is unwilling to help – and in any case the children ignore him. The consequent upheaval has a direct impact on the couple, whose relationship is put under strain.

The parents of the couple are reaching the age when they become seriously ill or die, and the strain imposed on the spouses, particularly if one parent has to come and live in the matrimonial home, may be considerable. The husband may be under stress at work, fighting the pressures of younger men who are after his position, and a raised level of irritability may be unloaded at home.

Finally the children leave home and this leaves an "empty nest" situation. The wife who is not working has relied on the children for support, and may now find she has to relate to her husband, who is a stranger to her.

Psychological Illness

The associated stress of the previous social factors may lead to a depressive illness. Indeed there is an increase in the incidence of depression at about the time of the menopause. One study has shown that one third of registered women aged forty-five to fifty-nine were likely to receive a prescription for a psychotropic drug (Skegg, 1977). In Dundee a study of women aged forty to fifty-four included five hundred and thirty-nine women. These women were divided into premenopausal, menopausal, up to five years postmenopausal, and six or more years postmenopausal. The menopausal group had the highest prevalence of probable psychiatric cases (Ballinger, 1975).

Ballinger's study was a postal questionnaire, and other studies have tended to show that the increase in psychiatric illness is related to age rather than specifically to the menopause. These authors have reached the conclusion that there is "no evidence that women are at greater risk of depression during the menopausal period, or that depressions occurring in this period have a distinct clinical pattern" (Weissman & Klerman, 1977).

Further research will clarify the conflict of these views. Nevertheless, when a depressive illness is present at or around the menopause, it is important to treat it promptly, otherwise the malaise, loss of sexual desire, and lack of energy will have an adverse impact on those couples whose marriages are vulnerable. A clear history will establish whether the partner has been subject to an affective disorder before and that this is a recurrence, whether the social events of this period are triggering the illness, or whether there is a mixture of menopausal and depressive symptoms. A combination of antidepressants and psychotherapy may be indicated, plus support for the husband.

Apart from specific disorders, paranoid illnesses are not uncommon in this age group, and may be associated with the menopause. In particular, morbid jealousy may emerge (see Chapter 10).

Psychosexual

The physical concomitants of vaginal dryness may lead some women to complain of vaginismus and the absence of any desire to be touched. But psychosexual difficulties should not be directly related to the loss of ovulation, for the accompanying hormones do not play a major determining factor in sexual intercourse. Indeed hormone replacement therapy does not improve libido.

There may be temporary abatement of sexual interest due to the presence of other symptoms which lead to general loss of interest or energy, apathy and indifference, but in general the menopause should not affect the sexual life of a woman, unless it is used as an excuse to avoid further intercourse when sex has been poor for many years prior to the menopause (Ballinger, 1975).

In some rare cases the menopause becomes the occasion for women to withdraw from sex. These are wives who have a strict view of sex and consider it as being exclusively for procreative purposes. When the possibility of new life ceases, then such a woman blocks sexual access to herself. The number of such people will probably get steadily less as the social and religious factors associating sex and reproduction become of lesser importance.

Indeed, the menopause may be a time when some women suffer a loss of confidence in their feminine identity. The specific and exclusive potential of procreation has now ceased. There is a certain sense of loss with the menopause, and psychodynamic writers have associated the loss with a depressive reaction. This may be true in some people, but the more general fear of losing one's feminine charms is likely to be more important. Such wives need reassurance that the loss of their procreative role does not interfere with their significance to their husbands. They may need extra affection and warmth to remove any lingering anxiety that they are unacceptable.

The majority of women negotiate the menopause without any difficulty and may feel liberated to proceed to the next third of their life. No longer concerned with the risks of pregnancy, their sexual life may take on a new lease of vigour. In these circumstances the relevant factor is the response of the husband. If he can take up the challenge, the couple proceed to the third phase of their marriage with their sexuality intact. From now on the possibilities of sex will largely be determined by the man. Most men continue sex in their fifties and sixties, but a small number become impotent and then coitus has to be replaced by physical affection.

Extramarital Activity

During the forties and fifties both men and women may undergo a crisis of sexual identity. These are the years when the ravages of time may erode sexual confidence. Extramarital activity may be no more than a transient event, often unbeknown to the spouse. When the activity is discovered, the trauma depends on its significance. If it is a casual affair implying little threat to the marriage, then after an initial traumatic response the couple will come to terms with it. If it is a prolonged and serious affair, then clearly it will threaten the marriage unless it is given up.

Some men and women are more vulnerable and find any extramarital activity intolerable, so that it arouses a degree of anxiety and insecurity out of all proportion to the seriousness of the affair. It is these spouses who refer themselves for counselling because they cannot accept the infidelity. They are often men and women with insecure attachments who are readily threatened by the possibility of loss, and an affair, however trivial, is considered by them to be a serious danger to their relationship. These people frequently appear unforgiving to the point where they drive their spouse to abandon the marriage, when the spouse originally had no such intention.

Kinsey (1948, 1953) calculated that 34 per cent of married men and 20 per cent of married women had extramarital sex. These figures include all such activity, which varies from one-night stands to serious affairs in which the marriage is at risk. Thus although adultery constitutes a threat to marriage, very often the affair which leads to divorce has been anticipated by a serious deterioration in the marital relationship.

In practice every extramarital affair has to be considered in detail. Is it a transient phenomenon or does it reflect a serious deterioration in the marriage? Is it a warning that the spouses are neglecting each other emotionally and sexually? Or is there a deep-rooted personality disorder? Depending on what emerges in the history, the counselling must try to answer the needs of the individual couple.

When extramarital relations are numerous, then clearly a personality disorder is involved. Very often such men and women are extremely insecure people with low self-esteem who need to be reassured repeatedly that they are wanted and appreciated. Such people need extensive individual help.

9. Alcoholism

Alcoholism is a major contribution to marital problems and ultimately to marital breakdown. It is estimated that twice as many marriages complicated by alcoholism end in divorce when compared to the general population marriage breakdown rates (Oppenheimer, 1984).

Alcoholism in marital pathology assumes a greater importance when it is realized that the number of alcoholics in Britain is rising. In a report from the DHSS (1976) the number of alcoholics was then calculated to be of the order of 500,000 people. The increase of drinking in young people and women has played a part in the general rise of alcoholics, who are currently calculated at over 1,300,000 men and women (Oppenheimer, 1984).

Divorce is not alcoholism's only adverse consequence on marriage. Alcoholics are prone to increased disease, falls, attempted suicide and – above all – a higher death rate, leaving behind a trail of widows (*Population Trends,* 1976).

Alcoholic Dependence Syndrome

Much has been written about the problem of alcoholism, and it is considered that genetic, physiological, biochemical, social and psychological factors play a part (Paton et al., 1984). Initially alcoholism was considered to be a disease, and such a powerful body as Alcoholics Anonymous backed the concept. The world authority on the subject, Jellinek (1952), also supported this concept. Such an idea comforted the alcoholic who felt that, since he was sick, he could not help his behaviour which was somehow excused by his "illness", and reassured the millions of other drinkers who felt that their genes, biology, social and psychological make-up were free from the disease elements and therefore they could drink with impunity. Unfortunately the work of epidemiologists and economists shows that the number of alcoholics rises with increased consumption (Paton et al., 1984), something that should not happen if there were physical factors that safeguard people from the disease.

As the concept of disease has fallen into disrepute, it has been replaced by that of dependence. The "Alcoholic Dependence Syndrome" was a term developed by Edward & Gross (1976). The word "syndrome" means the observable coincidence of phenomena. When one or more of these phenomena is involved, then problem drinking is present.

The syndrome has seven main characteristics. Firstly, there is a subjective feeling of compulsion to drink. Secondly, the dependent person needs to drink regularly to avoid withdrawal symptoms of nausea, morning shakes, bouts of amnesia and the inability to function. Men and women who are dependent on alcohol, finding themselves in situations where they cannot drink – such as being ill, entering hospital for an operation, going into prison – exhibit marked withdrawal symptoms. These people are not recognized as alcoholics and yet their regular drinking masks their alcoholic dependence. Thirdly, drinking is so important that it takes priority over all other activities. Such people *must* go to the pub, must have their drink at home, and they become very agitated if prevented from doing so. Their family responsibilities are neglected as precedence is given to drinking. Fourthly, the level of tolerance changes. The dependent person can drink more without getting drunk, which gives a false sense of security. Fifthly, the syndrome contains the feature that dependence is associated with repeated withdrawal symptoms such as early morning shaking, tremor and nausea. Sixthly, these withdrawal symptoms are reversed by further drinking; and seventhly, the syndrome can return after periods of abstinence. Edward & Gross (1976) suggest that the more dependent a person is on alcohol the less likely is he able to return to normal drinking.

Adverse Impact of Alcohol on Marriage

The adverse impact of alcohol on marriage is extensive, and of course can be, for long periods, far short of marital breakdown. The damage can range from social isolation to spouse conflict. The family with an alcoholic spouse becomes increasingly socially isolated. The husband who gets drunk in social situations both at home and when visiting friends is an acute embarrassment to his wife. He causes a scene by talking too much, too loudly, making rude interruptions, attacking friends and relatives and – in the end – becoming incapable of functioning. He has to be carried to the bedroom and is not a pretty sight. The embarrassment is particularly acute if the alcoholic is the wife. Repeated behaviour of this type leads to the reduction of invitations, and such a couple ultimately find themselves isolated.

Alcoholic dependence has an adverse effect on work. The alcoholic is unable to carry out his work, particularly on Mondays (Murray, 1975). Incompetence at work leads to dismissal, and the work record of alcoholics is markedly poor. Unemployment leads to family poverty, and a vicious circle is established between unemployment and further heavy drinking.

The presence of an alcoholic dependent parent may have, in the long run, adverse effects on the children. Time which should be spent with the children is taken up drinking or sleeping off the effects of drink. The associated quarrels of the parents frighten the children, who may remain awake at night, alert to the next fight between father and mother. The consequent stress may affect school work, cause regression, produce illness or lead to antisocial behaviour.

As far as the spouses are concerned, alcoholic dependence is a potent cause of violence. In a study of battered wives (Gayford, 1975), alcoholism was present in 75 per cent of the cases. Typically a man will go out drinking and return drunk. When drunk he will be highly irritable and the slightest criticism may spark off a row. During the row he may become abusive and violent. He will say things which are damaging and hurtful. He will strike his wife in the face with his fists, kick her and sometimes put his hands round her throat as if to strangle her. The results are painful and traumatic. The next morning he will remember little or nothing of what happened the night before.

Violence, however, can be exhibited by either spouse when drunk, and particularly when both are drunk. When that happens they may hurl abuse at each other as well as solid objects. Women will kick and scratch, and men use their fists. Often these scenes take place at night when alcohol, tiredness and sleep deprivation form a vicious circle.

The drunken husband can become sexually aroused but unable to perform because of associated impotence. In general women find a drunken man repellent, and will often refuse him in that state. Refusal may cause further anger and so trigger off violence.

It can be seen that a combination of social embarrassment, recurrent quarrels, absence of communication and intimacy, accompanied by poverty, damage to children and physical violence can lead to marital disharmony and finally to separation and divorce.

Response by Spouse

In a study by Oxford & Guthrie (1976), five responses of the wife were identified in coping with the alcoholic husband. The first is the safeguarding of the family interest; that is to say, the material and social needs of children and husband are protected by the wife, who does her best to shield her children from her alcoholic spouse. The second is a continuation of the first, and involves a gradual isolation of wife and children from husband. They run a life of their own, keeping out of the husband's way, ensuring that he is not provoked, agreeing with him when drunk and generally leaving him alone to his drink. Thirdly, the wife hits out. She is continuously attacking her husband for his drinking. She nags, criticizes, belittles, usually all to no avail. The husband learns to ignore her remarks and goes on drinking. Fourthly, the criticism is associated with hysterical behaviour, suicidal gestures, drinking herself and in general acting out her distress in various dramatic forms. And finally, the wife accepts the husband's drinking and tries to protect him from the consequences. She makes excuses for his social isolation. She makes excuses to his employers. She protects him from the criticism of friends and relatives.

But ultimately the wife may have had enough and simply departs with her children. This may occur early in the marriage or after many years.

Choice of Spouse

How do women come to choose alcoholic husbands? Early work derived from psychoanalytic theory suggested that such wives had disturbed personalities themselves, and married their alcoholic spouse because of unconscious needs.

A typology of such women was made by Whallen (1953), who described the Suffering Susan, the Controlling Catherine, the Wavering Winifred and the Punitive Polly. The suggestion implicit in this theory is that such women had personality disorders, particularly hostility, and used the alcoholism of their husbands to express their anger. This view fitted in with the general conceptualization of mate selection, in which like was meant to choose like for neurotic characteristics (Tharp, 1963). This theory has been criticized in general, and in the case of alcoholics a study using the MMPI inventory did not show particular disturbance in alcoholic wives compared with controls (Ballard, 1959).

Another view known as the Stress Theory (Paolini & McGrady, 1977) sees alcoholism as a total family problem, in which both individual and social factors play a part. This is a view which does not differ much from the Systems Theory approach, which sees alcoholic behaviour as a symptom which affects the whole family (Steinglass, 1971), and for which family therapy is advocated.

Patterns of Marriage and Alcoholism

One of the facts that has to be considered in the impact of alcohol is that some spouses are already heavy drinkers before the marriage whilst others became so after a number of years. Clearly, all the questions raised by the mate selection vary, depending on the pattern of marriage.

When the husband – and rarely the wife – is a heavy drinker prior to the marriage, then the question of selection of such a person raises important considerations. Why was such a person chosen? Is it because the wife's father or mother drank heavily, and she was no stranger to heavy drinking? Was the attraction motivated by a desire to change the partner? Was the attraction evoked by sympathy and/or compassion? Or is it due to dynamic factors, such as the wife expecting no better treatment? Clearly the factors for such a selection will be very different from the marriages where alcoholism develops later in the union.

The presence of heavy drinking from the very start means that conflict, violence and social disturbances start from the beginning of marriage. The wife may become disillusioned early in the marriage, and such presence of alcoholism may contribute to the heavy incidence of marital breakdown in the early years. Such a man spends most of his time in the pub. He comes home late for meals, ignores his wife, attempts to make love when drunk and, in a combination of rough and uncivilized behaviour, manages to alienate his wife very quickly.

The clinical evidence of heavy drinking in the teens and early twenties suggests that such people come from backgrounds with high alcohol consumption, suffer from a high level of anxiety or tension, are moody, and take alcohol to lift recurrent depression or rapidly become physically addicted. All these reasons carry a poor prognosis for sobriety, and those who drink heavily prior to marriage are poor marriage risks.

In the course of the marriage cycle the next stress period is the arrival of children, and heavy drinking may commence then. In particular, some wives who become post puerperally depressed may turn to drink to alleviate their symptoms.

As far as wives are concerned, heavy drinking may occur in a situation where they feel trapped in a marriage from which they wish to escape. The progressive development from emotional dependence to independence has been described as a normal process of growth in marriage. Thus, most wives assume increasing authority, independence and autonomy in the marriage with the passage of time. Some husbands, however, find the independence of their wives a threat and refuse to acknowledge it. They continue to exercise stringent authority over their wives, who increasingly feel prisoners in their marriage. These women may turn to drink to cope with their frustration and unhappiness. The alcohol may release their mounting hostility, and a vicious circle is thus established.

In this instance, and in many others, the unhappy wife who is drinking may be brought to the doctor to have her drinking "cured". The husband seizes on the drinking as the cause of his wife's dissatisfaction with the marriage, and in this way protects himself from seeing the cause in himself. Unless great care is taken, everybody else, including the marriage counsellor, accepts the drinking as the problem instead of as a symptom of the underlying marital difficulty, and fails to do justice to the latter.

In the forties the family is hard pressed by several social events. The children are becoming adolescents, with all the turmoil that this entails, the grandparents are becoming sick and dying, with the consequent stress on the spouses, there may be employment difficulties, particularly for the husband, and both spouses may worry about their appearance and sexuality with the advent of middle age. All these stresses may spark off excessive consumption of alcohol, particularly if these are associated with marital difficulties.

Doctors tend to see spouses who are drinking heavily because they have become depressed or anxious, and the presence of an underlying psychiatric illness should always be remembered.

In the fifties the children depart. This is a time of particular crisis for wives, particularly those who are unemployed and those who have a poor or distant relationship with their husband. Up till now they have felt needed by their offspring and the latter's departure makes them feel irrelevant and of little meaning. If their husbands are busy and successful, these wives feel they have no role to play in their lives, and a sense of emptiness overcomes them when the children finally go. Drink is not the only solution to this common dilemma, but it can be used to overcome the social and psychological emptiness, and gradually takes over as a crutch.

Marked marital difficulties, quite independently of the patterns described so far, can lead to heavy alcohol consumption, and the arrival of drinking often makes the marital problem worse.

Outcome

In a unique follow-up study of 99 male alcoholics over a period of 10-12 years (Oppenheimer, 1984), it was found that 18 had died – a mortality rate 2½ times in excess of the norm for this age group – 68 were alive and interviewed, and 13 were not interviewed but a great deal of data was acquired from them. A significant finding was also that 33 out of the 68 who were interviewed were separated or divorced. Of the 37 who had remained married, 22 had a good outcome as far as their drinking was concerned, and 15 a bad outcome. Of the 33 who were divorced, 20 had a bad outcome and 13 a good outcome. This study shows that the chances of remaining married are greater if drinking becomes controlled, but some marriages continue even with disastrous problems of drinking. In the divorce population a good outcome, as expected, is less frequent, but it can exist and the marriage still end in divorce, suggesting that divorce in the alcohol marriage is a reflection of both the drinking and the underlying marriage problem, either of which can contribute to marital breakdown.

Treatment of Alcoholism

The treatment of alcoholism is complex (Paton et al., 1984), and the conclusion is that there is no general approach for every alcoholic. Each person who is dependent on alcohol has to be assessed with respect to the motivation to stop drinking, the social circumstances, including the state of the marriage, and their psychological make-up. Treatment requires support, the particular help of Alcoholics Anonymous for those who can make use of it, drug therapy and behaviour therapy. Each alcoholic has to be helped through a programme that suits their needs.

The wife of the alcoholic husband needs a lot of support. If she wishes to stay in the marriage she has to learn how to avoid provocation, or useless arguments, to cope with the aloneness of her state, to avoid blaming herself for her husband's drinking, and to protect her children from its adverse effects.

But in the end, every wife who finds her husband's drinking destructive and intolerable must be helped to leave her husband, as the only way of saving herself and possibly him as well. Some husbands will only act if their wives depart, though this does not always follow. Some of them continue to drink and end up as pathetic chronic alcoholics. But the departure of the wife is a psychological reality which may motivate a proportion of husbands to change. The same, of course, applies to the husband faced with an alcoholic wife.

In those marriages where there is marital conflict and heavy drinking, it is vital to distinguish the primary problem. If the drinking is a reflection of the marital problem, then the latter must be tackled. If the drinking is the primary issue, this needs priority handling. Often the two are inextricably mixed with each other, and both need to be attended to simultaneously.

10. Aggression

In the normal course of events couples will argue with one another and may exchange verbal abuse: but that is the point where the aggression will usually stop. In a small percentage the aggression will increase to verbal and physical violence. It is very difficult to obtain estimates of the incidence of such violence. The occurrence of the isolated violent episode is probably far more common than is generally appreciated. A study by Gelles (1972) of eighty families in the U.S.A. with marked violence showed a 30 per cent incidence of at least one episode of violence in the controls. In cases of divorce, Levinger (1966) established that 37 per cent of women in the U.S.A. cited violence as grounds for divorce. In Britain cruelty used to be a prominent matrimonial offence, and it is now subsumed under the title of "unreasonable behaviour". At the extreme end of violence are to be found women who are battered by their husbands and who sustain multiple and recurrent physical traumata. The most extensive study of such wives was made by Gayford (1975), who studied one hundred of them in Britain. Other studies of violence-prone families have been made in the U.S.A. by Steinmetz (1980), Coleman (1980) and O'Brien (1971). What factors emerge from these studies?

Social Factors

The evidence suggests that violence is related to families and husbands with lower education, lower social class (although no social class is exempted) and low incomes (Gelles, 1972; Steinmetz, 1980; Coleman, 1980).

As far as work is concerned, the suggestion has been made that men who batter are under-achievers (O'Brien, 1971) and unemployed (Steinmetz, 1980). Unemployment is interpreted as lowering the self-esteem of the head of the household *vis-à-vis* the wife and the rest of the family. Such a person may operate with a feeling of being looked down on and criticized, and responds with an explosive rage. Wives were only violent when they achieved more and were frustrated by the poor performance of their husbands (Gelles, 1972).

Perhaps the feature that stands out most of all is that such men and their wives have experienced or witnessed violence in their parents' homes. Steinmetz (1980) puts forward the view that violence is a learned behaviour transmitted from one generation to the next. Gayford (1975) found that battered women often had aggressive fathers, and so had seen the same pattern of behaviour in their homes as children.

When does violence occur, and in which part of the house? Gelles (1972) found that violence was initiated in the bedroom by men, in the kitchen by women, in the living room by both, but no violence is recorded in the bathroom! It is tempting to speculate on the reasons for these sites. Clinical experience suggests that the bedroom is the site where sexual conflict is experienced frequently, with the man wanting sex and the wife refusing. A lesser but well known factor is that bed is often the place where husbands and wives talk and press for information about each other's behaviour. This can, of course, happen in the living room, but the presence of children and other members of the family often precludes an extensive conversation. However, once the couple have retired to bed the verbal battering can commence. Questions about infidelity, comparisons with previous lovers, or hostile feelings can all be poured out. The arguments begin late at night and can continue into the early hours of the morning, with tiredness and frustration ensuing. These lower self-control, and finally aggression is acted out in violence. Alternatively, a spouse leaves the matrimonial bed and sleeps in another room.

The kitchen is the wife's territory. In a situation where she feels beleaguered, this may be her only refuge. The husband comes into the kitchen and wants to talk, ask questions, become erotic, and touches his wife; she makes excuses that she is busy with the cooking, washing, etc. He persists and her anger rises. Finally she may take a knife and either threaten to or actually will attack him.

According to Gelles (1972), the evening between five and eleven-thirty is the most likely time for violence to erupt. It is the time when the couple have the maximum exposure to each other, when alcohol is most likely to be consumed and sexual conflict experienced. In the author's experience the weekends can also be highly traumatic.

Wives' Response

At the beginning of the study of violence, wives were considered in psychoanalytic terms to be masochistic and therefore to have a predilection to seek violence. This view is no longer accepted widely. It is true that women who suffer violence may seek help, but they may also stay for a long time in the battering situation and be reluctant to seek assistance. If asked they would deny that they enjoy the pain and the humiliation of being attacked, but nevertheless they remain in the situation for periods in excess of what the outside observer would consider justified. A high proportion of these women experienced violence themselves or saw it inflicted on their mothers; in other words, they were conditioned to it. As a result they suffer from a degree of learned hopelessness.

Part of the help that can be given in these situations is the raising of hope and self-esteem. These women are battered not only physically but emotionally. Their self-esteem is low and so are their expectations. They become resigned in their despair.

Not only are such women resigned in their despair but they often find themselves socially isolated, cut off from friends and relatives, often at the insistence of their husbands, and therefore removed from the normal social support of the community (Steinmetz, 1980).

But not all women are passive, indecisive, or feel helpless and hopeless. In Gayford's sample, which was admittedly biased towards seeking help, 57 per cent had sought help from social services, 32 per cent from police and probation services, 15 per cent from solicitors, and 6 per cent from Citizens' Advice Bureaux. Finally, a number of these wives found their way into a refuge. One would like to think that this would be the end of the problem, but often their husbands pursue them. These aggressive men are frequently emotionally dependent and, despite their aggressive behaviour, rely excessively on their wives for survival. Such is their level of panic when left alone that they do all they can to secure the return of their wives.

This dependence also explains the behaviour of these men at home. After a violent episode they are often contrite, and promise never to repeat it. They apologize profusely and make splendid promises about the future, which needless to say they do not keep. But wives remain patient for a long time before they take action.

Special Situations

Whilst violence may occur at any time during the marriage, there are certain circumstances which are more prone to lead to it than others. These include alcohol, pregnancy and jealousy.

Alcohol has a well known uninhibiting effect and is probably the commonest antecedent of violence. It is cited frequently in the literature (Steinmetz, 1980; Coleman, 1980; Mitchell, 1978). The usual pattern in England is for the man to go out in the evening to a pub and return inebriated. His speech is slurred, his movements unsteady and he smells of drink. He may ask for sex, and when refused become abusive. He may react to his wife's criticism of his state by a violent verbal and physical outburst. Aggression released by alcohol is dangerous, because the ordinary inhibiting feelings of guilt, concern and control are absent. An inebriated man is a prey to his emotions with little control over them. Under such circumstances the husband may be humoured to sleep or incited to violence. In the violent outburst he may utter the most savage and insulting remarks, and lash out. Sometimes these scenes become exceedingly bloody and the wife ends up in the casualty department of the local hospital needing a number of stitches. Often the man has no memory of the events next day. He will face the injuries he has caused with horror and disbelief. His wife will tell him what he said, which he will find unbelievable. Given, however, how common alcohol abuse is, it is not surprising that it contributes so much to family violence.

Pregnancy should be a time of anticipated joy, and usually this is how it is experienced. Nevertheless it is well known that it is a time which attracts violence (Steinmetz, 1980). There are various reasons why it should be so. The man may not want the pregnancy, and a physical attack on his wife is an expression of his hostility towards it and an attempt to destroy the baby. Pregnancy may cause an intense degree of anxiety. The father may dread the responsibility of fatherhood, doubting his capacity to cope or to love. This increased anxiety is associated with aggression, which is directed towards the wife. The coming baby may be experienced as an acute threat to the intimacy of the parents. The father may fantasize that the child will replace him in his wife's affection. Further unconscious anxieties about his own childhood may be aroused: if he felt neglected, rejected, or hurt then, the coming child may remind him of those painful experiences. The wife may restrict sexual intercourse, and the already anxious and angry husband may see such refusal as the ultimate rejection. Frequently the aggression is associated with a heightened level of anxiety and an accompanying level of aggression.

Envy and jealousy are common human experiences but it is the latter that can cause marked aggression. Jealousy is a situation in which either spouse suspects that the partner is being unfaithful. This suspicion may be justified but it equally may not be. Shakespeare's Othello catches the flavour of what has come to be described psychiatrically as morbid jealousy (Shepherd, 1961). This morbid jealousy syndrome may be experienced by either spouse, and is characterized by the conviction that the partner is being unfaithful. The "evidence" is provided in abundance. The wife will trace seminal stains in his underpants, find hairs in his clothes, smell the perfume in his shirts, interpret his movements as time spent with another woman, is certain that telephone calls are from "her" and may even hire detectives to trail her husband. In the authentic morbid jealousy syndrome all these beliefs assume the character of delusions. The wife is thus not open to reason, will not accept any explanations and will act out her fury with physical violence.

The husband will similarly be convinced of his wife's infidelity. He will have a long list of "reasons" why his suspicions are correct, and no defence on her part will be persuasive. Often such a husband will keep his wife up all hours of the night asking her questions about the non-existent lover. In sheer exhaustion the woman may give contradictory answers to the questions and these contradictions will be seized on as an excuse for further questioning. Finally, in sheer rage, the man may attempt to strangle his wife, calling her a "whore", "bitch", "prostitute" and other insulting names.

Physical and Psychological Factors

In addition to the social factors and the special situations associated with aggression, what else is known about the behaviour of such aggressive people?

Examination of electrical brain activity (E.E.G.) has shown that some 5–10 per cent of the general population have abnormal E.E.G. patterns. People who are prone to violence show an increased incidence of such abnormal rhythms. This well known phenomenon suggests that there is a physical factor connected with aggression, and there is little doubt clinically that some people are more prone to aggression than others.

This process is shown by a low threshold to frustration, something which aggressive people find very difficult to tolerate. Their limited ability is tested in such common situations as congested roads, waiting in queues, waiting in silence as others speak, or when in pain, tired or ill. At home frustration can rise when a spouse meets one's requests with denial, hostility, refusal and unwillingness to discuss matters. Men and women who find difficulty in expressing themselves with words are particularly handicapped. It is well known that women generally have a verbal facilitation which men do not possess. There are, of course, individual exceptions, but men often complain of being nagged. The spouse, usually the husband, who cannot express his feelings in words, becomes extremely frustrated and emotionally tense. Such a person may either act out his frustration physically, or turn to drink, which loosens his tongue and unfortunately his fists.

The frustration described above is due to the failure of obtaining reasonable satisfaction of one's needs. There is another form of frustration leading to aggression which is linked with self-esteem. The person with poor self-esteem has limited resources to withstand criticism. The man who is teased about his sexual performance, his work achievement, his financial wisdom, or his technical ability and who lacks confidence in himself, can soon explode, and so can the woman who is teased about her appearance or her faults. Men and women with a poor image of themselves are easily reduced to despair, and either respond with verbal vitriol or, if they cannot express themselves adequately, act out their frustration in physical assault.

Another extremely common psychological factor is anxiety. It is well documented that the presence of anxiety is usually linked with an increase in irritability. Men and women who are anxious tend to be moody, to snap and act impulsively and aggressively. Whatever the source of anxiety, the rise of aggression produces a vicious circle. The anxious person acts aggressively, and then feels further anxiety arising out of guilt which leads to further aggression, establishing a vicious circle.

The ultimate aggressivity is to be found in the person whom psychiatrists call a psychopath. Such a man or woman tends to be anxious, moody, impulsive, has low tolerance of frustration and a high level of aggressivity, and is often emotionally very depressed, lacks self-esteem and feels easily criticized. Where such a personality is present in a marriage the degree of violence is high.

Child Battering

Homes with a high incidence of aggression also have a higher incidence of child battering. The literature on child battering is enormous, but one of the best British studies is that of Smith et al. (1973, 1974, 1975).

As far as the social factors are concerned, Smith finds that such mothers are younger at the birth of the first baby than is average for the population, that battering is more common with the first and second child, and that such families show marked social pathology. There is frequently illegitimacy, premarital pregnancy, a missing father, marital conflict and a rejecting attitude to the child. Furthermore such families – as in those with wife battering – are socially isolated and do not have family support.

These mothers frequently come from the lower socio-economic groups, and have both a limited intelligence and an abnormal personality. Another study showed that, as with battered wives and their husbands, mothers who batter their children were themselves the subjects of neglect, physical punishment and battering (Isaacs, 1972).

When it comes to the childrearing practices of such mothers, they show great expectations of their children, whom they want to appear to be perfect. They must be neat and tidy, orderly, disciplined and behave excessively well. In this way they are seen to reflect well on the parents, who desperately need this reassurance. But this excessive demand is coupled with a lack of warmth and excessive punishment which is often physical. When the child is not on show, the parents are indifferent to his behaviour. Parents who batter are unpredictable in their demands, hostile and punitive.

Response to Aggression

The aggressive spouse or parent is in urgent need of help, but as is well known, they do not seek help, and it is only on indirect evidence that the presence of battering emerges. G.P.s, health visitors and nurses, should be on their guard for any physical injury which is explained away as an accident, or when there are repetitive bruises or injuries. In all these situations the question of the origin of the injury should be relentlessly pursued.

If battering is found to occur in spouses, then clearly marital help is needed. If the husband refuses to seek help, the wife should be counselled. In general she should be given the opportunity to ventilate her feelings, to learn that whoever is supporting her will not desert her but instead will raise her self-esteem, confidence and assertiveness so that she can stand up to her husband. If the husband refuses to curtail his behaviour, the wife should consider temporary separation. She may be afraid of this because she has nowhere to go, has no money, is afraid of her husband, is terrified of surviving alone and sometimes feels blackmailed that, if she leaves her husband, he will commit suicide or disintegrate. She should be given practical support of alternative accommodation, the encouragement that life can be lived outside the home, and the reassurance that it is time to depart so that the husband can face the challenge of growing up. All this cannot be achieved in five minutes: it needs patience, perseverance and support.

Often when the wife actually leaves, it is the husband who breaks down. It is he who cannot cope and who has been hiding his immaturity behind his wife's willingness to put up with his limitations. When a battered wife is being counselled, it should be no surprise to find that as she gains confidence and assertiveness it is her husband who collapses, so that ultimately both need marital counselling.

In this mutual help the husband is found to be insecure, unable to express his fears, particularly of being abandoned and the constant dread of losing his wife to somebody who is better than he is. When the battering ceases the wife can summon up the courage to support her husband in his insecurity, building up his confidence and self-esteem so that he does not feel easily rejected. The husband too has to learn to avoid alcohol and to be supportive of his wife. Initially the couple will rely on the encouragement and support they will get from whoever is acting as counsellor. This support does not need prolonged sessions. Frequent reassurance, so that the couple know they have someone to rely on, is often all that is needed.

As far as child battering is concerned, the mother needs a good deal of help. Sometimes the child may need to be separated from her or the father; but even then the parents need to be counselled on the basis of raising their self-esteem, reducing their expectations of the child and giving them the feeling that they are no longer alone and unsupported. The management of these families is part of the basic training of the readers of this book, and so only an outline of the basics has been given.

Section 3

11. Introduction to Therapy

Given that a marriage is in distress, what can be done to help it? Initially the only form of assistance available was dynamic-orientated therapy. Subsequently two other forms of therapy have become available, namely behaviour therapy and systems theory. In this chapter a brief introduction will be given to each, and in subsequent ones dynamic and behaviour therapy will be described in greater detail.

Dynamic Therapy

Dynamic therapy in Britain has been based on object-relations theory, which has depended on many British-orientated therapists, including Klein (1959) and Fairbairn (1967), and which was firmly established by the work of Dicks (1967). The basic tenets of the theory are that the child introjects, takes in, both the positive and the negative aspects of its relationship with either parent. Both aspects become part of the unconscious and some are suppressed, particularly the hostile feelings. The suppression takes place through denial, splitting-off, idealization, and other defence mechanisms, but the feelings remain part of the unconscious.

In marriage the partner is selected for social and conscious reasons, but also, the theory claims, for unconscious reasons which contain both positive and negative intrapsychic feelings. It is the negative, hostile ones that cause the trouble. In the process of intimacy the spouse projects onto the spouse (projective identification) all the suppressed, denied, repudiated parts of the unconscious. In this way the spouse becomes the recipient of hostile feelings which belonged to parents, and are now relived in the spouse. But the mechanism is unconscious, the projecting spouse is not aware of what he is doing, and as a result there is a hostile interaction which does not belong to the reality of the current situation.

Dynamic theory aims at clarifying projections, coping with the anxiety created by raising to consciousness the repressed, integrating love and anger, and transforming a relationship from fantasy to reality. A great deal of work has been done in this area, and a basic awareness of its principles is extremely helpful in theory.

Behaviour Therapy

Dynamic theory goes back to the 1940s, and was primarily a British invention, although American workers have accepted and used it. Behaviour theory started some twenty-five years later in America, and has spread to Britain. Behaviour therapy has no similar complicated theory to that of the dynamic approach, but it includes the approach of Skinner (1953) and the social exchange theories of Homans (1950) and Thibaut & Kelley (1959).

Behaviour therapy is in many ways familiar to everyone, because it contains traditional basic human attitudes which consist of rewarding behaviour that is pleasing in order to increase its frequency, and punishing undesirable behaviour with the intention of reducing it.

Behaviour therapy thus depends on principles of reinforcement that increase or maintain the behaviour desired, and punishment that extinguishes undesirable behaviour. There are two types of reinforcement, positive and negative. Positive reinforcement is something we want and will work hard to get; in the case of marriage it includes such things as affection, sex, approval. We will do all the things that please the partner in order to get the rewards we want. Negative reinforcement appears on the surface as a contradiction, but it refers to a rewarding situation which is based on the removal of something unpleasant, such as, for example, nagging, or in non-marital terms, toothache.

Punishment is expressed by offering an unpleasant or aversive response to a particular form of behaviour. The second form of punishment is to withhold something which is highly desirable.

Finally, in the range of punishment but not exactly identical with it, is found coercion. Here spouses feel compelled to comply with unwanted behaviour in order to stop the harassment. In terms of short-term relief the harassment is stopped and the spouse gets what he wants, but in the long term such compliance leads to frustration, anger and hostility, and may prepare the ground for ultimate refusal.

Behaviour therapy aims to turn punitive, critical, aversive behaviour into something positive and mutually rewarding, by increasing the behaviour that pleases and reducing the parts which displease. In its theory and execution it has an elegant simplicity, and is making rapid advances in the whole field of therapy.

Systems Theory

Systems theory originated in the U.S.A. and has come into its own in family therapy. Its origins are not in the world of psychology and psychiatry, but its postulates are derived from mathematics and physics. Systems theory sees the family as a system characterized by wholeness, which means that "every part of the system is related to its fellow parts, so that a change in one part will cause a change in all of them, i.e. the system behaves as one inseparable whole". The second characteristic is that of equifinality, which means that "in a circular and self-modifying system results are not determined so much by initial conditions as by the nature of the process for the system's parameters. The same results may spring from different origins because it is the nature of the organization which is determinant." The third characteristic is feedback loops, in which the loops are circular with each response being determined by the one before (Watzlawick, 1967).

Systems theory implies that the couple and the children are part of a whole organization, in which change in one will affect all the others. It is a very good way of looking at the boundaries of the various members of the family. Too much dependence, the absence of independence, too much control by parents on children, and other such boundary confusions can be handled by systems theory. Family therapy has developed extensively in this country, but so far the origin and emphasis of the work is child-orientated, whereas the previous two approaches are primarily concerned with the couple.

12. Taking a History

NEWARK COMMUNITY
MENTAL HEALTH TEAM
SOCIAL SERVICES
RECEIVED
MAR 1989

The description of how to take a history is an ideal, and the details will vary with the individual worker. Counsellors usually try to see a couple together in their office. In fact health visitors, nurses or doctors may initially see one partner alone, sometimes in their own home. The particular points relevant to listening to one spouse will be considered later in the chapter. At this stage it is assumed that both partners are coming for the first time to the office of the counsellor.

Office

It is important that the "office" should be a place where the couple feel relaxed. If, for example, there is a video machine with a camera, this should be explained, and at all times the permission of the couple to video them, whether for their own therapeutic help or for teaching purposes, must be obtained. The placing of chairs should be adjusted so that the couple sit near each other, with the counsellor facing them, preferably with no table between the counsellor and the couple. They should be welcomed, asked to sit down, and the counsellor should explain that a history will be taken. This history can be written on paper or taped. If taped, permission should be asked and, of course, whether the history is recorded on paper or on tape, confidentiality should be preserved. One or the other partner may object to a history-taking, but an effort to overcome this objection should be made. Not only are the details of the first interview vital for the couple, who later on can be reminded of the progress they have made, but if the marriage proceeds to divorce the consultation may become relevant material for legal requirements.

Having tried to make the couple comfortable, relaxed and at ease, the counsellor makes a habit of taking the history on a sheet of paper which he keeps on his knees. He looks at the couple and says, "I understand you have come to see me because you have some marital problems." Even this simple statement may be contradicted. Either spouse may take the opportunity to state that they did not want to come, feel it is a waste of time, but have come at the insistence of their partner. Such information is already very revealing. Either you cannot expect much co-operation from the unwilling partner, or advance notice is being given that the relationship is over and the presence of that partner is merely a matter of ritual.

In fact such an introduction may warn the counsellor that the purpose of the visit is not to receive counselling for the improvement of the marriage, but to inform the counsellor and the partner that the marriage is concluded. The unwilling spouse has come to hand over their partner to the responsibility of the counsellor, so that she/he can look after them.

Assuming that the couple have come with the genuine desire to improve their marriage, then I proceed as follows. After the initial opening remarks I add, "Before going into the details of your difficulties I would like to know how long you have been married/lived together, how old you are, how many children you have, their sex and ages, whether this is your first marriage or a subsequent one, your address and the nature of your work." The information is fundamental and often not recorded.

Then I want to see who opens the proceedings, and

therefore record "H" for husband, "W" for wife, and my initials against what I say. The story begins to unfold. Before going into the details of the story it is important to consider the approach of the counsellor.

Counsellor

Anyone listening to marital problems will repeatedly hear similar broad outlines. Essentially couples complain of unmet needs and unacceptable behaviour, accompanied by negative feelings. The counsellor has heard it all before. In fact no marriage story is exactly the same as another, and it is vital that the counsellor not only makes the couple feel they are unique, but that he/she approaches each marriage with total openness, freshness and the capacity to be surprised, and communicates to the couple the fact that there is nobody else like them. Individuals will say repeatedly, "You have heard it all before", "There is nothing new", "You have been bored with the same old story", "If you are bored, stop me." The couple need to be listened to in such a way that, by the time they leave, they feel truly understood.

This means that the counsellor must approach every couple free from other preoccupations. He must ensure no interruption, such as telephone calls, disturbs the time with them. Nothing kills the empathy of the dialogue as much as the interruption of the telephone. Elsewhere I have stated, "The counsellor . . . needs to convey the feeling that he/she is experienced in the subject but is prepared to make a new journey with every couple and follow their particular signposts, discovering what is important to them. The approach to counselling needs to be that of a readiness to receive whatever is revealed and to treat it with skill, sensitivity, care and an original approach, so that no impression is given that the couple are the end-products of a factory process" (Dominian, 1984).

Some twenty years ago workers described the characteristics of facilitating counsellors as non-possessive warmth, genuineness and accurate empathy (Truaz & Carkhuff, 1967). These characteristics remain a permanent part of therapy. "Non-possessive warmth" means that the counsellor is relaxed and friendly, but in no way takes away the freedom, initiative and individuality of either spouse. He is not a parent who demands obedience, but the marriage remains a matter for the couple themselves to decide on. "Genuineness" has already been hinted at, namely that, although skill is used, the counsellor is truly honest and sincere in whatever he says or does. He really cares for the couple, is honest with both his negative and positive remarks, does not pretend nor does he manipulate. He does not have to reveal fully his thoughts or feelings. He should communicate what is helpful and not show off that he is familiar with the theory of marital pathology. "Accurate empathy" is probably the most important aspect of counselling. The counsellor must read accurately the meaning, both intellectual and affective, which spouses express. One of the reasons why they are in difficulty is that they have been unable to read each other accurately, and that is what the counsellor has to do for them. He has to listen to what they are saying and translate its meaning, a meaning which may not always be clear to them and is certainly not clear to the spouse. A counsellor must be a feeling person, and the greater his sensitivity in becoming an accurate translator of the inner world of the spouse, the more successful he will be. In a study of behaviour therapy it was shown that these qualities emphasized by Truaz & Carkhuff made a significant difference to the work done (Mickelson & Stevic, 1971).

Although the advantages of seeing a couple together are considerable, so are the risks. The counsellor may come to like one partner and dislike the other. Technically he may identify with one and have negative feelings towards the other. This will become obvious by his comments and will have a disastrous effect on the counselling. Consciously he must remain neutral and yet unconsciously he may sympathize with either and show this by his approach. This can and does happen, and so the counsellor must be on his guard and be constantly monitoring his remarks. It is helpful to remember that even the most attacked spouse often behaves in a way that encourages the other to perpetuate the behaviour. Sympathy for the victim must be tempered by the reality that the victim often provokes the aggressor, and sometimes has unconscious reasons for maintaining the situation unchanged. Thus the counsellor always has good reasons to suspect his bias; there is always the other side to the matter.

But handling both parties fairly is not easy. Very often both of the couple are determined to make the counsellor their ally against the spouse, and it takes a lot of skill to keep the balance of availability and goodwill to both. Of course, not every remark has to be balanced between the partners. What has to be shown is their positive and negative characteristics, the way they love and hate, the manner in which they irritate and appreciate their spouse. The counsellor is there to clarify, explain and put the relationship into perspective, moving from a position in which the couple have categorized each other into "good" and "bad" into one where moral characterization recedes and the behaviour of the couple is understood either in terms of the past, i.e. childhood, or the present established vicious circles, or both. It is imperative for the counselling to change the terms of the relationship from judgemental accusations to mutual understanding of why certain kinds of behaviour occur. There are very few people who are deliberately nasty or hateful, even though that is how they are seen by their partner. It is the task of the counsellor, who is not enmeshed in these negative feelings, to help the couple to see that moral judgements do not do justice to the reality of the situation.

Two American authors (O'Leary & Turkewitz, 1978) have stressed that the role of the counsellor is to increase the rapport of the couple by focusing on behaviour that can be changed and by teaching the couple to show serious concern for each other's feelings which they have hitherto dismissed. In other words, if the counsellor shows that he is paying clear attention to the feelings of the couple, to their behaviour and not to their judgemental attitudes, they will do the same to each other. Clearly the counsellor must listen and observe simultaneously. Listening means paying attention to what is being said and to the feelings that accompany the statements. The statements are accompanied by feelings of anger, sorrow, distress, excitement and agitation, and they are responded to by anger, agreement, disagreement, surprise, denial, concern or indifference. The counsellor has to note who is doing the telling and in what manner. He has further to observe whether the couple are talking to each other or only to the counsellor, and, of course, there are body messages as well. Are they shaking their heads in denial or in approval? Do they look up to the ceiling as if to call God as a witness for the lies told? Are they waving their hands, wagging their fingers? Sometimes the couple are taken by complete surprise at what they are hearing, which is a revelation to them.

All this has to be noted, and if necessary commented upon. But the important thing is to relate the feelings to the facts. What is causing the feelings? What are the circumstances which arouse such passion or indifference?

The counsellor has to listen, observe and note the behaviour of the couple in front of him, both in respect to the accounts given and the way they are relating to each other. The latter is very important, for he can verify with his own observations the styles of interaction between the couple.

The Interview

The counsellor notes who starts the story and writes down the details of what is being said. There follows the account of the partners, and in this way the first ten minutes or more are taken up by the complaints. As far as possible the counsellor should not interrupt, except when the couple cannot begin at all, in which case he says, "There are five areas in marriage, the social, emotional, sexual, intellectual and spiritual. The most important are the emotional and sexual ones. Perhaps you would like to tell me something about the way you feel regarding your emotional and sexual life." Usually the couple will then begin to talk, and the counsellor lets them take over until they have finished the first round of remarks. If he sees that they are simply repeating the complaints he then interrupts, but the first real interruption after the initial ten to twenty minutes is to make a summary of what he has heard.

"As far as I can see," he says, "you, John, find that Jean is not letting you make love to her. She says she is not interested in sex. You are angry and upset with the situation, which has been dragging on for a long time. There are arguments and quarrels in bed, and you have told her she is frigid and she should see a doctor. There is nothing wrong with you, but you are sure there is something wrong with her. You are fed up. You, Jean, complain that John spends all the time in his office. He goes early, does not see the children, and gets home late. He is tired, hardly says a word, has his meal and then watches TV. He does not speak to you, and when you ask what has happened during the day he says, 'Nothing special'. This infuriates you. You feel that you are there only to cook and wash. You are angry, and the last thing you want is sex." The counsellor then asks the couple whether his summary is an accurate reflection of what is happening. If it is not, then the couple are encouraged to go on with the details.

It is important for the counsellor to ask for exact details. Couples exaggerate in order to make an impression. Thus, if the husband is supposed to be mean, then the actual housekeeping sum should be established. If sex is infrequent, its exact frequency should be agreed. In this way the counsellor can be objective, factual, non-judgemental in his summaries. Gradually he is creating an atmosphere where the couple can express their feelings openly and without the anxiety of retaliation.

Another aspect of the interview is for the counsellor to enquire about and to stress those aspects of the relationship that are satisfactory. The idea is to bring into the summary not only objectivity about the complaints but also a mention of those aspects of the relationship that are going well.

When a summary has been agreed upon it is time to proceed with the enquiry regarding the couple's background. It is important to find out something about the marriage of their parents, its quality, durability and how they related to their father, mother and siblings. From the psychoanalytical point of view, but in fact from every theoretical angle, the early life and the relationship of the spouses to their family of origin gives information about their growth, maturation, identity, relationship to parents and therefore the sort of expectations they have of their spouse.

With this new round of information the counsellor formulates a new summary in which the present and the past are amalgamated. The couple begin to see how their past is influencing the present, and how unconscious attitudes are defining their attitudes to the spouse.

At this stage the counsellor will proceed, according to his

theoretical framework, to discuss with the couple what he considers to be the important issues which are going to be examined in psychoanalytical or behaviouristic terms, an account of which will be given in subsequent chapters.

Whatever theoretical assumptions are made, the couple need to go away from the first session with a reasonably clear idea of the nature of their problems. They need to feel understood and also to be given clear instructions as to when they will come back, how often and what they have to do in the meantime. All this means advice, which until recently was anathema to marriage counselling. Increasingly, however, it is being realized that only a few couples can cope with a strict psychodynamic approach, and that the majority need some very clear notion of what happened in the interview, what the problem is, how they are to tackle it, and when they are to be seen again.

All this applies to the couples who are clearly orientated to marriage counselling. As already suggested, couples come to counselling with mixed attitudes, and part of the skill of the counsellor is to convert the hesitant spouse into a more optimistic partner who will agree to come again. In some instances, however, it is clear that one spouse does not wish to proceed with reconciliation, and having come feels he has done his duty. Such people should not be pressed to return against their will, but the counsellor should offer his availability if circumstances change.

Single Spouses

Often only one spouse will come. Such a visit is welcomed, and the person is listened to. The evidence is that it is usually the wife who wants to talk (Brannen & Collard, 1982). It is she who feels the urgency of the situation. She may present herself as depressed, battered, in doubt about her sanity or in despair.

Her history is taken in the same way as above, but it is vital that her account does not remain the only one. Her spouse's account should be sought. The counsellor will be told that the husband will not come, and sometimes this is true. In fact a letter of invitation, couched in the following terms, "Your wife has come to see me about your marital difficulties. She is in great distress and I am sure you would like to help her. In any case, there are always two sides to a marriage and I would very much like to hear your version of what is happening", often gets a positive response.

But in any case, even if the husband does not come, work can be done with the wife alone. She can be helped to understand that, whatever her complaints, marital conflict involves two people and, in addition to being helped to understand her husband's behaviour in a non-judgemental way, her own contribution to the conflict can be elucidated. In the early days of behaviour therapy wives were treated alone (Goldstein, 1971), but this has been abandoned as a deliberate policy, although sometimes it may be necessary.

Unless it is necessary, the wife should not be treated with antidepressants or tranquillizers, although these may have their place. She should be supported and helped to feel that she has a problem, and that she is not going mad. If her husband sees that the help she is getting is altering her behaviour towards him, he may feel left out and may want to participate. In any case she is no longer alone and can be helped either to improve her marriage or, if that is not possible, to establish a separate life.

The danger of seeing a spouse alone is the prominent one of identifying with their cause and providing them with ammunition to attack their partner. This should never happen. It is imperative that the absent spouse is given the benefit of the doubt and treated as positively as possible. If the spouse who attends finds such a positive reception of their partner unacceptable they will cease to come, but if their intention is to preserve the marriage, the positive attitude of the counsellor will be welcomed.

13. Dynamic Marital Therapy

Dynamic marital therapy is based primarily on the concept that human beings have the capacity to form a series of intimate relationships. The first one is between the child and its parents, and often the second one is between spouses. Thus marriage is frequently the second act of a two-act play. In addition to these two intimate relationships, there are deep friendships. What is special about subsequent intimate relationships? In later intimacy the other person – in the case of marriage, the spouse – is experienced in a similar way to the parental figures. When the relationship with the parent has been distorted, then the same distortion can be repeated with the spouse. In Chapter 2 we saw the stages through which a child develops emotionally: it forms a bond with mother and then father, and then, within this bond, trust, reliance, affection and love are experienced. Within the same bond the worth of the child develops as parents approve its activities and give it a feeling of self-esteem. All this is happening in the closeness of the relationship. But the child needs to separate from parents and find its own independence. If independence is not encouraged, then it remains emotionally dependent on the parents who continue to make decisions, take the initiative, allay anxiety and act on its behalf. Finally in the course of its relationship with the parents the child can and does feel angry when it is disappointed, frustrated, anxious or rejected.

The experiences of childhood, particularly the negative ones, are often rendered unconscious, and repressed or suppressed. They are removed from consciousness but remain part of the personality, and then when intimacy is reintroduced in marriage the suppressed returns, and the spouse now experiences the partner with all the negative feelings of deprivation, dependence or lack of self-esteem which were experienced with the parents. Thus a knowledge of the relationship with key parental figures is an essential part of history-taking, so that feelings towards a spouse can be evaluated and a distinction made between those that belong justifiably to the partner and those that are foisted on them as part of the transference from the past.

One of the key theorists of this approach to marital therapy has been H.V. Dicks (1967), who formulated theories that a spouse can either select a partner who is a straightforward displacement of a parental figure, or choose a fantasy figure, the sort of ideal replacement. In traditional Freudian terms, the wife's transference should be the characteristics of her father, and for the husband those of his mother. This, of course, can and does happen, but in practice the transference can be with either parent, the choice depending on who has been the significant key person emotionally.

When does the spouse begin to experience the partner in the same way as the parental figure? The experience can happen from the very beginning of marriage, or when there is a crisis. Marriages go through critical phases when children first arrive, at time of illness, when a parent dies, at the menopause, when the children depart, or when the security of the couple is threatened as, for example, at times of unemployment. During these periods the need for security, reassurance, affection, love and sex is accentuated, and the capacity of the partner to rise to the occasion can be severely tested.

Deprivation

It is on these occasions that a wife or a husband becomes aware of what is missing in the relationship. For example, when the first baby arrives the stress on the life of the woman increases. Most husbands rally with help in the home, reassurance over any of the mother's anxiety about the baby, and sexual appreciation to show that the pregnancy has not diminished their feelings, together with an easing of demands, attempting to ensure that the care of the baby does not deny the privacy and intimacy of the couple's life. When this care is not observed, the wife complains that her husband does not help, continues his inordinate demands, keeps his outside contacts while leaving her alone and isolated at home, demands sex, and is not generally aware of the presence of a third party. Thus the arrival of the child reveals the pronounced limitation of the caring capacity in the spouse. When attention is paid to the details of the wife's parental home, it may be found that her father had the same characteristics of being an indifferent care-taker. The return of the suppressed not only reveals that the wife has married someone similar to her father, but it also unleashes a hostility which was present towards the father though not conscious. Now the husband becomes the target of the disappointment of affection, coupled with the hostility for feeling let down. The same sequence of events may take place when the need for affection arises. A repeated story is that of a wife who is deeply concerned at the lingering fatal disease of her favourite parent. During this period she expects extra support from her husband, and it is often forthcoming but, when it is not, then the deprivation can be considerable and so is the anger that accompanies the feeling of being let down. Illness produces the same reaction. A wife may feel devastated when, during an attack of flu, her husband continues to expect her to cook the food, clean the house and look after the children.

Crises highlight the needs of couples and the capacity of partners to compensate, but when a person has been truly deprived of affection in childhood then their needs dominate the marriage. They marry someone from whom they expect not only to receive affection and support as in an ordinary marriage, but also the extra attention that was missed in childhood. Such a person may be short of the sense of trust, the feeling of being wanted and appreciated. The extremely deprived will be aware of their need to be reassured often and deeply. In fact when they marry a stable, mature, loving person, they get exactly the treatment they want and so receive healing in their marriage. If they marry someone who is as deprived as they are, then both spouses will be competing for attention, and the union of two extremely deprived individuals does not produce a stable relationship.

Dependence

At the heart of human growth lies the gradual separation of child from parent, so that by the end of the second decade the young person can stand on their own, socially and emotionally. At the extreme end of this continuum are to be found young people who cannot leave home because they are frightened to live separate lives. These are men and women referred to psychiatrists. But another solution is to go from a dependent relationship at home to a dependent relationship in marriage. The woman who has failed to grow up marries an assertive, extravagant, dominant husband and is happy to rely on him for decisions and initiative. For a number of years all goes well, and then imperceptibly she begins to find that she has gained in confidence, security and maturity. She wants now to take far greater charge of her life. Such a husband may be willing to let her learn to drive, go to work, have her own bank account, her own set of friends, help him with his work, etc. But if the husband finds her development a threat to his power, if he feels cautious about delegating authority, then he will refuse to concede to her wishes. This makes her angry and ultimately leads her to feel a prisoner in her husband's hands. Her anger escalates and there are arguments and quarrels, and she may withdraw from sex. This antagonizes the husband, and by the time the couple are seen they are in a state of war.

The growth of emotional dependence into independence in marriage contributes to one of the commonest patterns of marital conflict when the dominant partner is unwilling to let go the hold over the spouse. After extended efforts the spouse, often the wife, decides to leave, and does so. This may in fact lead to a crisis for the husband. The man who appears strong is not so. When his wife departs he finds himself lost and is full of anxiety. In fact it often happens that the wife's departure reveals the concealed dependence of the husband. It is he who needs his wife much more than she needs him. If a happy outcome is to emerge from therapy, the husband must come to see his dependence and needs, which have been hidden behind the dominance he exerted.

Another term for such a relationship is a collusion. The husband is really entirely dependent but will not acknowledge it. His unwillingness to accept it is helped by the wife's dependence, which brings out his dominant, powerful, assertive characteristics. Such a couple are locked in a relationship in which their true selves dare not be revealed for a number of years. But a change in one, often the wife, destroys the unconscious collusion and the other has to change as well. The change demanded from the husband is extremely threatening, mobilizing anxiety, and is therefore resisted. This is the stage where the couple seek help and, in the absence of a dynamic understanding of the relationship, it is not easy to explain to them what has been happening.

Self-esteem

In the course of development, parents not only facilitate their children with the capacity to develop their intelligence, skills, activities and verbal fluency, but make them feel that their achievements are good. In this way the self-esteem develops. This self-esteem may be impaired when children do not feel loved, are excessively criticized, are ignored, do not receive attention, or are excessively anxious and do not register the affirmation received from parents. These men and women grow up lacking self-esteem. They do not feel they can achieve anything of value. If they are creative, they do not trust their achievements. They lack confidence, they feel inferior and do not believe that anybody wants or appreciates them. Such men and women unconsciously choose partners who fit in with their feelings by being excessively critical. The need to be criticized and put down is met in this way, and this is another pattern of collusion. But gradually the feeling of self-rejection changes. The person who feels inferior changes. Now they want to be appreciated and, as with dependence, the outcome of the marriage depends on the ability of the partner to alter. This is often difficult and in these circumstances what has often to be done is to help the person with the growing self-esteem to reach a degree of self-confidence so that they do not mind being criticized. They can learn to ignore the criticism, and gradually, when the negative spouse finds that his remarks no longer have an emotional impact, he gradually ceases to behave in this way.

Idealization

Another mechanism that operates in dynamic therapy is the process by which men and women who have wounded backgrounds tend to see their partner in rosy or idealized terms. The chosen man or woman will be different from anybody else: they will be protective, caring, loving, sexually arousing, and all the limitations of the parents will be made up. The idealization, of course, soon turns out to be unreal. What happens next is not a reappraisal with lesser expectations, but an upsurge of rage at being let down. This rage and anger existed at home and was suppressed. Now the disappointment brings out the pent-up fury from the past, which is released upon the spouse.

There is a good deal of evidence already presented that marital happiness drops from the beginning of marriage. The distortion brought by idealization is one of the many reasons for this fall.

Technique

Numerous books have been written about psychotherapy with marital couples, and here only an outline can be given. The therapist aims to help the couple by observing their emotional interaction. By watching them in action he can see the way they are feeling about each other. They may feel dependent and say little, agree easily and avoid any expressions of anger. Their deprivation may be expressed in a long list of unmet needs. Their lack of self-esteem may bring out deep complaints about the way they are criticized. All these feelings may be objectively accurate. The spouse may be acting in the way complained of. Equally the spouse may deny acting in the critical manner, and the evidence may support this. The therapist will then interpret to one or both partners how their emotions are based on displaced feelings from a parental figure. For example, a wife may feel that her husband never listens to her, in the same way that she could never talk to her mother, who always told her that she was busy and could she leave her story for later on. But the therapist can see in the interaction that the husband does listen and most carefully. This false interpretation of the situation or projection is interpreted to the wife. She can see in action what she is doing. Transferences are not only one way. Both spouses can be projecting the past onto their partner, in which case confusion reigns as reality is missing from the situation.

When a spouse has his or her behaviour interpreted, for example when he is shown to be angry with his wife in the same way that he felt angry with mother or father but had not expressed it in childhood, the awareness of the angry feelings may cause anxiety or guilt. When a spouse's particular problem is excessive anger towards the partner, he has to become aware of it, feel it, include any accompanying anxiety or guilt and then gradually accept the anger without fearing that he is going to destroy the person he loves.

A good deal of dynamic interpretation is related to helping partners recognize their negative feelings towards each other, distinguish what is merited and what is a transfer from the past, accept their angry feelings instead of splitting them off as they have done up till now, and yet in the end feel they can love and be loved. For some people this process takes a long time.

So far the transference of feelings interpreted is between spouses. But there is also a transference between spouses and the therapist. This can be a positive transference, in which the therapist now becomes an idealized parental figure with whom an alliance is being sought against the spouse, or a negative transference in which all the hostile feelings of the spouse are projected onto the therapist.

In the positive situation the therapist will be on his guard and recognize that a repeat situation from childhood is being re-enacted. The spouse allies with the therapist as a parental figure as happened in childhood, e.g. daughter combined with father/mother against the other parent. Such triangular situations are particularly likely to happen in therapy and they should be watched with care. Sometimes the positive transference is on a one-to-one basis, and the therapist becomes the depriving parent from whom a lot of love is expected. The spouse is ignored and the partner directs all their attention to the therapist, from whom approval and care is expected. Once against this situation should be recognized and it is the therapist's task to understand and interpret it.

In the negative situation one or both spouses feel that the therapist does not like them, rejects them, is critical of them, and the rejection of the past is relived. Such hostility towards the therapist is a useful tool of interpretation to help the spouse realize their unconscious feelings of rejection and their internalized sense of being unlovable.

Thus the therapist has to monitor the feelings that the couple have for one another and assess reality from fantasy, and also do the same for himself. The latter process should be easier because he should know what he feels, and be able clearly to distinguish his own feelings from those that are projected onto him.

As the couple move away from mutual anger they can come to realize that they have mixed or ambivalent feelings towards their partner: they both love and are angry with them. The object of therapy is to integrate these two feelings and not let their anger destroy each other. This process of recognizing the mixture of feelings and accepting them, i.e. living with the limitations of the spouse without extravagant rage, takes time. But the ultimate object of therapy is to move the spouse away from childhood experience, recognize reality as it is currently, appreciate the partner's good points and tolerate the bad ones, recognize that love will be associated with approved behaviour and anger with disapproved, and that both can be felt and expressed without fear that irreparable damage will be done when anger is expressed.

So far the transference has been in one direction, either towards the spouse or towards the therapist. But what about the feelings of the therapist towards the couple? This is counter transference. The therapist has to guard against his own positive and negative feelings. He must ensure that they do not lead to taking sides. He must remain scrupulously fair. But when the therapy has been going for some time and the relationship with the couple is established, he can use his own feelings to illustrate a point. He can say, for example, that if he was the husband or wife and was faced with a particular remark, he too would be angry. Or, if he tries to reply to one partner and is constantly interrupted, he can show that he feels frustrated at being unable to have his say, just as the partner feels at home. In other words, the counter transference is used to illustrate the manner of interaction between the spouses.

Dynamic therapy for marriage is a useful tool and, when its basic principles are applied in suitable situations, a great deal of clarification can be achieved. It has been the main therapeutic tool for marriage in Britain, but now behaviour therapy is also increasingly used, and this will be considered next.

14. Behavioural Marital Therapy

The first approach to marital therapy was the dynamic treatment of the couple as individuals. Very soon the dynamic emphasis shifted to seeing the couple together and, of course, in family therapy all the members of the family are included. As indicated in the previous chapter, the dynamic approach has been the most extensively used in Britain. But behavioural therapy has made considerable advances in the last fifteen years, and for some problems has a simple and attractive elegance. Unlike dynamic theory, the behavioural approach has no extensive theoretical basis. It is based on the belief that in effective marriage there is a high level of mutually rewarding behaviour and the opposite obtains in stressful ones. This mutuality of rewards is based on the social theory of Thibaut & Kelley (1959). Behaviour therapy owes a great deal to the pioneering work of Stuart (1969) and Liberman (1970) in the U.S.A, and Crow (1973, 1978) in Britain. The work of these authors set in motion Behavioural Marital Therapy (BMT). For a detailed and excellent summary of the subject, Chapter 9 of *The Handbook of Marriage and Marital Therapy* can be consulted (Sholevar, 1981).

In behavioural terms consequences which tend to increase the probability of a behaviour they have followed are called positive reinforcers, and those that involve avoidance or escape from aversive conditions are negative reinforcers. In both cases the behaviour reinforced will increase. Thus if a husband comes home and is greeted with a kiss and a hug, he will keep coming home as often as possible to have this rewarding behaviour. If he comes home late and is nagged, he will try to come home early to avoid the nagging, and that is still a reinforcement, but now called a negative reinforcement because it is based on the desire to escape something unpleasant. At the heart of behavioural marital therapy is the change of behaviour so that positive reinforcers are increased and both partners get what they want from each other.

Punishment has the opposite effect. It is meant to decrease behaviour which is found unacceptable. In more technical terms, it involves consequences which tend to decrease the probability that the behaviour they follow will occur in the future. Punishment can be active in the form of critical remarks or passive through withholding gratifying behaviour such as sex, food, affection. A main thrust of behavioural marital therapy is to use the therapist as an agent who brings about a change in the behaviour of the couple so that gratification is increased and punishment reduced. Whilst the therapist will help by advice, acting as a model, teach new ways, the work of behavioural marital therapy has to be done by the couple, and this work is primarily change in behaviour. How is this done?

The therapist listens to the complaints and his first task is to tell the couple that it is not useful or constructive to use moral judgements against one another. "He is selfish", "She is lazy", are global remarks which perpetuate the hostility and put the spouses on the defensive. These remarks have to be translated into concrete characteristics. "He is selfish" needs to become a list of exact wishes of what the wife would wish her husband to do. This may include helping with the children, i.e. putting them to bed; with the chores, i.e. laying and clearing the table, washing the dishes; coming home earlier, taking the family out, visiting her relatives, and so on. "She is lazy" is transformed into a series of wishes in which the husband expresses the desire that his wife keeps the house cleaner or tidier, gets up to give the children their breakfast, cooks his favourite dishes, irons his shirts, etc. The wishes are mutual. The two spouses want things from each other, and the idea is that responsibility for change is accepted by both, and each will try to please the other. This conversion of general complaints to specific desires means that both partners know clearly and precisely what the other requires of them.

Another feature that is frequently present in the exchange between spouses is the insistence of dragging the past into the discussion. "He is so lazy . . . He has always been lazy . . . From the very start I could see what sort of chap he was. My mother said he was no good, but I would not believe her. I soon found out she was right. He has never been any good." Now the attack is not only global but extends all the way to the beginning of marriage. Such an attack ensures that the husband has always been defined as a bad sort. In this description he has no hope of changing, he is damned for ever. Behavioural marital therapy aims to move from the past to the future. At the end of the session the couple must get the feeling that change is possible. The therapist can say, "I know you feel that your husband/wife cannot change, but this is not the case. People do change with encouragement and assistance. And in any case if he did not want to change he would not be here."

So far the therapist aims to move the discussion from global to concrete instances of behaviour, from negative to positive attitudes, from the past to the future. Next he will look at the leisure pattern of the couple. A recurrent complaint in marital difficulties is that the couple have little time together. The excuses are extensive. They are too busy or too tired during the week, they have young children, or have different interests. Intimacy is a vital component of marriage. During the period of togetherness a couple renew their awareness of each other, the pleasure of feeling recognized, wanted and appreciated, and the good feelings generated often pave the way for sexual intercourse. In the course of my work I advise couples to allocate one evening each week for each other and do with it what they mutually like. If they have common interests, they can go to the cinema, to the theatre, to the pub, or if their interests are disparate they can take turns to do the things that please each other. One group of therapists (Liberman, Wheeler & Sanders, 1976) suggest to their couples that they each have individual leisure, that they do things together, have contact with other couples who are happily married, and have family outings. Leisure time together is not the only form of togetherness I advise. Another period of togetherness is a daily contact of anything between a quarter of an hour to half an hour when the couple sit and talk to each other about the way the day has gone and the problems that have arisen and that need to be solved. American therapists have called these periods "executive time" (Liberman, Wheeler & Sanders, 1976), "administration sessions" (Weiss et al., 1973) and "family meetings " (Gottman et al., 1976).

Thus the therapist aims to help the couple undertake mutually pleasing concrete tasks which are positive. The husband is asked to do whatever the wife wants, the wife is similarly asked by the husband. This reciprocal negotiation needs motivation and mutual undertaking, and the tasks need to be manageable and practised regularly. It is the homework of the couple. The range of reciprocal tasks recommended are few at the beginning, perhaps one, e.g. that the husband comes home early from work and that the wife greets him at the door, and then little by little the mutual tasks increase until the couple reach a point where they are behaving towards each other in a mutually acceptable manner.

The impression may be given that reciprocal negotiation is a rather cold, bartering process, devoid of feelings. In reality it is nothing of the sort. Couples who are at war with each other, arguing and fighting, have lost the sense of being positive. Clearly they want to stay together, otherwise they would go not for counselling but to a divorce lawyer. What reciprocal negotiation helps to achieve is to retrace their steps. At the time of presentation they are deeply angry with one another, but they are still bonded. The reformation of their behaviour into clear, concrete, achievable, positive objectives means that they can recapture a sense of mutual caring. Out of the positive behaviour there emerge caring feelings and the marriage is restructured into positive lines. Of course, in order for this to be achieved there must be a minimum of goodwill left, despite the hostile atmosphere. But often marital conflict involves two people who cannot stand the behaviour of each other but who would like very much to change. They cannot do so because they are locked in vicious circles in which the negative behaviour of one is responded to by a defensive reaction in the other. When the mutual behaviour changes, feelings also change for the better.

Communication

A principal feature of behavioural marital therapy is the ability of two people to communicate with each other satisfactorily. Couple after couple come for help, and when they are asked what the problem is they reply, "We cannot talk to each other." Communication usually stops because the spouses get too angry, and their attempts to talk to each other end in a row. When this has happened several times they give up talking to each other. Some couples come for help after many years of failure to talk to each other. Like behaviour, communication needs to be positive and mutually rewarding.

The first thing the therapist has to do is to make sure that both partners actually talk. Sometimes one spouse does all the talking for both, and the partner says very little or nothing at all. As already described, it is my practice to ensure that both husband and wife have their say. If one party starts a monologue, giving the other little chance to interact, I stop them and say to the partner, "How do you feel about what you have heard?" I then wait until the silent partner has his/her say.

But it is not sufficient to make sure that both partners actually express their thoughts. It is important that they are taught to listen to each other. Sometimes all that happens is that one partner talks and the other is simply waiting impatiently to intervene, in order to deny, contradict or simply return to the list of complaints. This is not empathetic listening. Spouses have to learn to listen to each other, both in terms of the thoughts they are expressing and of the feelings that accompany them. Listening carefully means that when one spouse stops speaking the other can render a feedback. They can make remarks which show they have understood what the other spouse is thinking and feeling.

It is the task of the therapist to teach the couple the essentials of speaking in turn, listening to each other and then learning to agree or to disagree. So often when a couple cannot accept each other's views they feel that their partner is not merely presenting a different approach but that in doing so they are actively hitting out, negating, putting down or attacking the other. Differences of opinion cannot be expressed without feeling attacked, leading to such frequent statements as, "Whatever I say is wrong . . . I have only to open my mouth and she/he will find fault with what I say . . . all our discussions end in an argument in which I can never be right . . . it is no use talking; he/she only listens to what they want to hear . . ."

Not only do the couple have to learn to speak and listen to each other accurately, respond back to each other sensitively and accept differences without feeling attacked, but they have to learn to speak to each other in a relevant manner. That means they must not switch from one topic to another:

Wife You are always late coming home.

Husband That's an exaggeration. I have been home the whole of last week in good time.

Wife And when you come home all you do is read the paper.

Husband That's not true either . . . I help to put Johnny to bed.

Wife And you are always on the phone with your job.

Husband I made one call in the last two weeks.

Wife You have an answer for everything . . .

In this typical conversation the wife ignores every justifying reply and simply moves from one accusation to another. The exchange has to be noticed by the therapist and remarked upon. The therapist points out that her husband is not allowed to defend himself, that she exaggerates, shifts the ground and basically has a negative image of him.

In fact communication can go wrong for any of the following reasons (Sholevar, 1981):

1. Spouses attack only and do not tell their partner what they want.
2. One spouse does describe accurately their wishes, but the other does not recognize the signal accurately.
3. Information is sent and received accurately, but the sender demands instead of requesting.
4. The spouse wants to please but does not do it clearly enough.
5. The spouse thinks he is pleasing but fails to realize that

the partner is not pleased.

6. A partner just does not register the gratification offered by their spouse.

7. A partner perceives the gratification but does not acknowledge it, thus gradually stopping the positive messages.

What is the way to overcome these difficulties? One worker (Guerney, 1977) suggests the following programme which is called Relationship Enhancement:

1. Often spouses irritate each other because they state their views in a dogmatic manner, e.g. "I know this is true . . . I am sure that what I said is right and everyone would agree with me . . ." Instead of being so categorical spouses can say to each other, "It seems to me . . . I think, but, of course, I may be wrong . . ." In this way the partner is not allowed to retaliate and say, "You know everything . . . you can never be wrong . . ."

2. Couples can talk to each other factually. They do not express their feelings. Instead they can express feelings such as "I am worried . . . I am hurt. I am angry . . . I enjoy this . . .", and then join the feelings with the thought. "I worry when you come home late and don't ring me", instead of being angry and irritable when the spouse is late.

3. There should be an attempt to be positive and not negative. If criticism is to be made, then it should be first initiated with something positive, e.g. "I know you help me with the washing, but you do it so clumsily and you break so many things that in the end it is not worth the trouble . . . I appreciate you bringing a cup of tea in the morning but you wake me up so early that I can hardly enjoy it . . ."

4. Guerney emphasizes the point that has been repeatedly made already, namely, it is essential for couples to be specific

about their thoughts and feelings. Instead of being general, "I wish you were nice to me . . .", a more accurate communication should be, "I like you to hug me when we sit together at night."

5. When criticism is made it is vital that spouses should acknowledge each other's predicament, e.g. "I know you are tired when you come home but I would appreciate it if we could talk to each other about the important things that happened during the day."

Having communicated as clearly as possible, a couple may be left with a real difference of opinion which has to be resolved. How can this problem be solved? The best way of solving a problem is to do it in an atmosphere which is free of mutual criticism and hostility. The couple should aim at a positive interaction, leading to an agreed exchange of what the problem is. When there is goodwill, the problem can be solved by requesting a change. This change is now effected out of concern, care and love. If change is effected, the spouse should not be expected both to change and like the change. That is too much. Initially the request is met, and perhaps later on feelings can change as well. Even more important is to promise that, if a change takes place on this occasion, then a reciprocal change may take place on another one.

At other times change does not occur simply on request. Rather the couple agree carefully on all the advantages and disadvantages of the conflicting behaviour. They let reason and reality have the last word. If a spouse changes on this basis, it is vital to make sure that the change is not seen as a victory/defeat. The change of the behaviour is accepted on an objective basis. The maximum information about feelings and thoughts is exchanged, and the couple base their conclusion on the result of the combination of the two.

Sometimes a radical change cannot be effected. The wife

may want far more help in the house, and the husband cannot accept this. Instead of an outright rejection of help, one solution may be of partial help, a little initial move in the right direction and, if this is appreciated and goes well, then the help may be increased.

Behavioural marital therapy involves good communication and effective co-operation. It is particularly useful when there are marked arguments, quarrels and misunderstandings, but a minimum of a basic relationship remains present.

15. Sexual Therapy

As with the other therapeutic approaches, sexual therapy has many books to its credit, of which Masters & Johnson (1970), Kaplan (1974) and Bancroft (1983) are some of the major contributions, with Bancroft being the leading author in Britain. The initiators of the most widely used sexual therapy are Masters & Johnson, whilst Kaplan has amplified and developed this work. Readers who want detailed knowledge of the subject are referred to these works. The ease and wide applicability of the behaviourally derived therapies may suggest that sexual help is a cold, therapeutic practice. In fact it does not work like that. Skilled practitioners know that for intercourse to work body and feelings have to co-operate and be in harmony with each other, and even more important the couple concerned should be having a good relationship. Sex cannot easily happen in the presence of anger, hostility, mistrust, marked anxiety or guilt. The only way to bypass feelings is to use a prostitute who provides a physical channel without the involvement of emotions, and some use prostitutes for precisely this reason.

Relationship of the Couple

Couples come for sexual therapy, presenting a sexual symptom such as lack of desire, when in fact the main problem is their relationship. Repeatedly men and women find they cannot have sex with each other, only to learn that they can respond extremely well in an extramarital relationship. In the extramarital encounter they find themselves wanted and appreciated, they can have sexual intercourse and enjoy it. Sometimes sexual help is sought within marriage when an extramarital relationship is pursued and there is no intention of giving it up. In this instance it is essential to eliminate the infidelity and concentrate on the marriage if progress is to be made.

Thus at the very outset the commitment and relationship of the couple needs to be assessed. It cannot be repeated too often that sex is declined when a spouse feels angry or guilty and, of course – and this is not to be forgotten – when they are depressed. In any of these circumstances the appropriate marital counselling has first to take place. When the problem is a straightforward depression then antidepressants may be considered. Usually the conflict is a straightforward one in which feelings of resentment and frustration have reached such a pitch that intercourse becomes unacceptable. Alternatively the tension in the relationship rises to such a height that the wife cannot relax sufficiently to have intercourse, or the husband's erectile capacity fails. When anxiety and tension reach such a degree it may continue long after the original conflict is resolved. In that case the anxiety needs help in its own right.

Emotional Background

Husbands often consider coitus as an isolated event taking place whenever the circumstances permit. Wives, on the other hand, see sexual intercourse as the culmination of a day where the emotional background has been right. Thus wives want to feel in touch with their spouses through communication, expression of feelings, general awareness, giving them the feeling that they are recognized, wanted and appreciated prior to having sexual intercourse. If a man leaves early in the morning, comes home late, eats and then goggles at television, he has hardly any time for his wife as a person, but he nevertheless expects her to respond to him sexually in bed. Many wives submit to this type of intercourse which in time becomes mechanical and loses its emotional content, so that gradually its frequency is reduced, not for physiological, but for psychological reasons. Ultimately the rate becomes once every month or few months, and then the couple come for help because of apparent lack of sexual interest. The fact is that the physical has to relate to the emotional, and if the latter disappears from married life the physical wanes too.

Not only can the emotional background during the day be arid, but too often the actual preparation for intercourse is minimal or absent. Most of the time the initiative comes from one spouse, often the husband, sometimes the wife, and so there is no reciprocity of interest. After the initiative has been taken there is often no preparation in terms of cuddling, kissing and caressing, but a straightforward penis-vagina penetration. This approach works for the man but not for the woman. The subsequent experience lacks enjoyment and may be completed with absence of orgasm on the part of the wife, particularly when the husband is quick in reaching his climax.

It cannot be emphasized too much that the aim of intercourse is a celebration. It is true that it is a recurrent minor celebration, but, although sex can fulfil several purposes, it is ultimately an expression of love and it should be approached in such a way that the emotional arousal leads to the complementary physical one. Physical arousal without feelings is incomplete.

After some years of marriage, with the advent of children, fatigue and the pressures of survival, sex can be relegated to the bottom of the list of priorities. It is up to the therapist to remind the couple of the elementary precautions that are needed to revitalize this experience, and sometimes nothing more is needed.

Childhood

The grown-up person's sexual behaviour is influenced considerably by what was learned in childhood. The learning can be divided into two parts. The first is what was seen and heard, and the second, what was experienced.

Children see how their parents show affection to one another. This can be overt and demonstrative. Parents hug and kiss one another in front of the children, who see and learn from them. Sometimes just the opposite, the distressing experience of physical and verbal violence, is witnessed and imitated. Parents can be appreciative of one another or persistently highly critical; this is also learned. Children not only see but hear. They hear the activities in the bedroom, and they often know intuitively whether the experience of intercourse is satisfactory for the parent or accompanied by shouts of "Leave off . . ., not tonight . . ., what again . . ., not when you shout like that . . ."

They experience affection from parents, particularly in terms of touch. They can be kissed and hugged, sat on the knees of parents, stroked or generally made a fuss of. On the other hand they may have parents who do not touch. Parents may show their affection with words of praise, or they may be persistently critical. All this is learned and becomes the basis of how affection is, or is not, demonstrated in marriage.

The home atmosphere can be open to sexual topics or a conspiracy of silence may exist in which the subject is not discussed. If it is discussed then it can be limited to its procreative potential: "Sex is for producing children only" had been the upbringing of centuries and still influences some women who, having had children, do not see the need for any further sexual intercourse. Sex may also be associated with guilt feelings linked through religious teaching.

All this is within the normal range of experience. We know that some children are subjected to incest, sexual exhibitionism from adults, rape, and other sexual traumata. The way each sexual trauma was handled will either cushion the distress or enhance it. Some women in particular emerge from childhood with marked sexual wounds inflicted by parents and relatives, and they relive these feelings in marriage.

The whole range of childhood experiences may be revealed in the history-taking or unfold in the process of sexual therapy. The therapist has the task of education, advice, reassurance and cognitive change, so that feelings and attitudes may gradually change.

Sexual Problems

According to Bancroft (1983) the commonest male sexual difficulties are those of impotence and premature ejaculation, and more rarely of low sexual interest and retarded or absent ejaculation. The commonest female difficulties are lack of enjoyment followed by low interest, and less often of vaginismus and dyspareunia.

In general, after looking at a couple's relationship, attitude to sex, and particular feelings of guilt or aversion, they are then encouraged to pursue a modified Masters & Johnson programme with the following stages.

Stage I

The couple are invited to abstain completely from sexual intercourse or sexual stimulation. In this stage they are encouraged to touch, stroke and massage one another. I advise the couple to have a bath, feel relaxed, go to bed (preferably naked when this is acceptable) and take it in turns to stroke each other in the non-genital areas. First one spouse does it and then the other. The couple tell each other what parts of their body they enjoy being touched and those they do not. In this stage the couple relearn to be in physical touch with each other, to avoid the anxiety of having to have intercourse, and in cases where the woman has reached the stage where she cannot be touched she learns afresh how to experience this without the fear that intercourse will ensue. In the course of touching each other, the husband may get an erection and the wife become sexually aroused. The couple are instructed to ignore these sensations and to concentrate on touching.

The couple are seen after this stage and the experience reviewed. It is important to identify any problems, in particular the confusion between affectionate and erotic touch. Some partners react to all touch as a signal of subsequent sex, and the slightest touch produces anxiety and tension. In this exercise they learn to distinguish and to enjoy affectionate touch.

Stage II

After the couple are happy with the sensation stage, they can proceed to erotic touch. The man can stroke and stimulate all the areas which evoke sexual, erotic response, such as the breasts, nipples, the vagina and the clitoris, and the woman stimulates the man's erotogenic zones and the penis. The pattern is the same and the couple take it in turn to stimulate each other. They also inform each other what they like and dislike, and they try to increase the pleasure given. Sexual arousal is much more likely to occur at this stage, but again intercourse is avoided. However, for the man who suffers from premature ejaculation this may be the moment when the wife helps him to overcome this difficulty. He tells her that he is feeling the desire to ejaculate, and she in turn places two forefingers on top of the tip of the penis and the thumb underneath and she squeezes until the desire to ejaculate disappears. By carrying out the squeeze action repeatedly the man learns gradually to control the desire to ejaculate.

The couple return for evaluation of this phase. Any individual difficulties in connection with the touch of the genital area are examined and considered. Some erotic parts feel forbidden initially, and the fears and doubts of the individual have to be overcome. There are women who find holding the penis repugnant, and there are men who have no idea either of the actual anatomy or the excitation possibilities of their wife's vagina. All these difficulties can be discussed and overcome.

Stage III

This is the stage when the couple are instructed to proceed further to actual penetration. The position for penetration is a matter for discussion, and what is most acceptable to the couple is preferred, but I often encourage the husband to lie on his back and the wife to come on top of him. This position places a good deal more responsibility on the wife, and allows the husband with erectile or ejaculation problems to relax and simply concentrate on penetration, which occurs passively for him. The couple are instructed to enjoy penetration, but not to proceed to the friction of intercourse. This is meant to teach the maximal relaxation for the partners and to accustom them to further excitation which is learned in a controlled way. If the husband becomes excited and feels he is about to ejaculate, he withdraws his penis and is helped by his wife with the squeeze technique. When the pressure to ejaculate abates then the penis is reintroduced to the vagina.

The couple are invited to discuss their feelings about this stage and any difficulties are sorted out.

Stage IV

The final stage is the same as Stage III, but with the addition of the friction leading to orgasm.

This modified Masters & Johnson approach has been used extensively throughout the world, with each practitioner making slight adjustments to the overall model. In couples whose relationship is good and who have no individual difficulties, this therapy can be very efficacious. The trouble is that it appears so easy that far too many therapists prescribe it without all the other counselling precautions outlined in this chapter. The author frequently sees couples who have gone to a sex therapist and have been given this advice when in fact they needed marital counselling.

Absence of Intercourse

There are situations when intercourse is not possible through illness or permanent impotence. If the couple still desire each other sexually they may find they can stimulate each other to orgasm provided they find this aesthetically and morally acceptable. In addition, I advise couples to remember the powerful impact of affectionate touch through hugging, kissing and caressing each other. In this way physical closeness is attained and the sense of belonging frequently reached.

Sexual Variations

The usual basis of sexual arousal is the presence of a person of the opposite sex. There are, however, men and women who find a person of their own sex sexually attractive and this delineates the group of exclusive homosexuals. The Kinsey findings indicate that 4 per cent of white males are exclusively homosexual, and that the figure for women is about 1 per cent (Kinsey, 1948, 1953). Such exclusive homosexuals do not marry, and present different problems. But some homosexuals do marry either from social pressure, in an attempt to cure themselves, or because they want to have a family. Some of these marriages end very early on when the homosexual partner simply leaves. Others proceed for many years of marriage, during which the wife is not aware of her husband's predilection, and then at a time of stress the husband may have a homosexual affair, to his wife's great surprise.

Although brave attempts to treat homosexuality have been made, both dynamically and behaviourally, it is generally recognized that such attempts are not very successful. In the end a wife may have to learn to live with a husband who has these inclinations, but a lot of counselling may be needed to make the necessary adjustment.

After homosexuality, another group of common variations are sexual fetishes. In this case, an inanimate object becomes a source of sexual arousal. Fetishes are widespread, usually involve the husband, and may include rubber, fur, high heels, female underclothes, the colour black, etc. These fetishes are common and harmless. They constitute a problem, however, when sexual arousal can only be elicited in the presence of the object. Thus a husband may insist that his wife goes to bed wearing a leather mackintosh, as being the only basis on which he can get a sexual erection. It is surprising how accommodating wives can be, but sometimes they have a strong feeling that the fetish is more important than they are. In this case counselling is needed to raise the level of awareness of the wife as a person, and when indicated an attempt can be made to desensitize the husband to the fetish.

Sado-masochism is strictly a pattern of sexual arousal in which some people can only get excited when they receive pain, either physical or mental (masochism) or when they inflict pain, physically or mentally (sadism). The extreme variations of sado-masochism are clearly pathological and extremely rare. There are, however, men and women who enjoy submission to their partner, or in turn to be the dominant spouse. These patterns, when mutually acceptable, can enhance the sexual life of a couple.

Another variation is transvestism. In this case it is often the man who wants to cross-dress, that is, wear feminine clothes, particularly underclothes, or a complete feminine outfit. Sometimes wives know of this desire before marriage and collude with their husband. They help them to dress in this fashion, tolerate their behaviour at home and have coitus with them cross-dressed. Others are not aware of this desire and come across it accidentally. After an initial shock they either adapt or find the practice unacceptable. Sometimes the desire can be altered behaviourally, but with all variations the person concerned is usually not anxious to change the behaviour.

Sometimes wives discover sexy magazines hidden in the house, and clearly read by the husband. Such a magazine may shock a woman, who finds the fact that her husband needs to depend on such literature an affront to her own position. Men buy such magazines for a variety of reasons. Their libido may be low, they may be preoccupied with some fetish, they are sexually immature, or they are addicted to such literature. Such a predicament needs counselling to try to understand the husband's motives and help to overcome the problem.

Finally, there is the wife who is confronted with her husband's illegal sexual behaviour, whether it is exhibitionism, incest or, rarely, rape. In all these situations the couple have to be helped to understand it. Sometimes this is easy, at others extremely difficult. Often such men are emotionally markedly immature and need support to grow emotionally. On other occasions such immaturity is related to poor sexual life in the marriage. Whatever the reason, such offences bring acute problems to the wife. If she is the only person who knows of the husband's activity, what should she do? In the case of incest, how can she protect the children? It is imperative that such a family should be seen as a whole and wherever necessary marital help for the couple given.

NEWARK COMMUNITY
MENTAL HEALTH TEAM
SOCIAL SERVICES
RECEIVED
MAR 1989

16. Staying or Going

Frequently the therapist is asked whether a spouse should stay in the marriage or leave for separation or divorce. Such a request means that a final decision has not been made. If it had, the spouse would have gone straight to the solicitor. What should the response be? I make it a rule never to advise a person to stay or to go. First of all, this is a personal decision and must not be made by anybody else. Secondly, if an answer is given in either direction, the therapist becomes responsible for it and then is accused if things go wrong. Thirdly, the partner of the spouse who seeks advice may be solidly against the separation and put subsequent blame on the therapist. For all these reasons – but particularly the first one – no advice should be offered. But this does not mean that no help can be given.

Here the author finds his own scheme particularly useful. He invites the spouses to look at the social, emotional, sexual, intellectual and spiritual parameters of the relationship, and they can then trace together what viability there is left in the marriage.

Social

He asks whether the couple spend any time together, visit their relatives or friends, entertain or are entertained. Sometimes the reply is that the only time they can relate is when they are in company. This is significant information, suggesting that they cannot cope with personal closeness or intimacy. They can only function in social situations where they are expected to display the roles of being husband and wife but not the substance.

Further questioning is directed to the duration of estrangement. Is it of recent origin or has it been going on for years? If the alienation is long-standing, the chances of reconciliation are limited.

Emotional

In this dimension the capacity to show and receive affection is the principal issue. Affection does not need to be demonstrated in any one way. It can be physical, verbal or in action, and what needs to be established is whether it really does appear in any form. Sometimes the complaint is that the husband keeps lavishing on the wife gifts such as flowers, rings, jewellery, clothes, etc., whereas what she wants is genuine affection, rather than objects which make *her* feel an object.

Sexual

Here the enquiry leads to the frequency of sexual intercourse. Often what is disclosed is that intercourse has not taken place for years. What is particularly significant is the man or woman who no longer wants to be touched, and does not want to overcome this difficulty. They are sure they cannot, and do not want to be touched ever again by their partner.

A major issue is the question of infidelity. Is infidelity worthy of marital breakdown? Clearly not, for millions of couples go through the experience and overcome the distress. But there is the question of repeated infidelity, and also acts of infidelity which suggest that the spouse wants to have the partner and the third party. Should this be accepted?

Intellectual

Is there any sharing of common interests or opinions? Can the couple see eye to eye on common subjects? Or have the partners reached an irreconcilable diversity of outlook?

Spiritual

The same applies to the spiritual dimension. Is this dimension important to the spouse? Is the partner indifferent or hostile to it? Is there any common belief? Do the couple disagree violently about the upbringing of the children in a particular faith?

At the end of the examination the spouse who is making the enquiry will be able to see whether there is any viability left in the marriage. If the couple do nothing together, share no affection or sexual life and are indifferent to each other intellectually and spiritually, then clearly no relationship is left. But suppose pockets of relationship are left? Clearly the decision must be the spouse's, but increasingly nowadays the significant parameters are the emotional and the sexual ones.

This is in fact what distinguishes contemporary marriages from those of previous generations. In the past many couples often decided to stay in a marriage in the absence of any viability and in the particular absence of affection and sex. Today the emphasis is on a minimum of fulfilment and, when this is missing, then it is often considered time to go.

Violence

In the analysis just made the criterion of marital breakdown was an absence of mutual involvement or the presence of extensive indifference. This is often the pattern presented. But there is an alternative one. This is punctuated by frequent and severe quarrels, arguments and the presence of violence. This violence may be physical or emotional amounting to what the law sees as cruelty. It is remarkable how much cruelty spouses – and in particular the wife – will put up with from each other. Even after admission to a refuge for battered wives, some wives still want to return to their previous situation. The motives for staying in such a hostile environment are complex and have been summarily dismissed in the past by the phrase "masochistic". This is too easy an explanation and, as has already been shown, the personalities of these women show multiple social and psychological traits which make them vulnerable to such treatment. The ultimate decision must, of course, be left to the spouse, but objectively I make it clear to a couple or an individual that violence is unacceptable as a form of civilized behaviour. If it is tolerated, then this is up to the person concerned, but the denial of the basic love which is the object of marriage has to be expressed.

Therapy/Counselling

Spouses coming for advice on the possible termination of their marriage often arrive singly and ask that their partner should not be told of the visit. Against such a background it is up to the therapist/counsellor to ask whether help had been sought. Sometimes it has, often it has not. The wife, who is the most frequent enquirer, will often say that her husband simply will not come. An attempt should be made, even at this stage, to see whether help can be given. An offer should be made to write and invite the husband. Sometimes a great deal can be achieved, to the surprise of the wife.

Temporary Separation

A question asked as often as that of permanent separation or divorce is that of temporary separation. A husband or wife may feel that they cannot tolerate the situation any further, and want a temporary separation. Temporary separations have not been studied extensively, but one such study in the U.S.A. has shown that after a year of temporary separation the vast majority become permanent (Bloom, 1977). In my clinical experience I find that a temporary separation may give such relief from the impossible situation that there is no desire to return. Equally, a temporary separation is a time of reflection, when the poverty of the marriage is finally seriously recognized and a decision against returning made. Or the person who separates may have been frightened to consider living alone. Once they have achieved this and find they can cope, then their fears disappear and they take the final plunge to separate.

These reasons often suggest that temporary separations are a prelude to permanent ones, though this does not always happen. If the separated couple stay in contact, see each other and continue to look at their problems in a constructive manner, then temporary separations can lead to reconciliation.

Recurrent Departures

There are marriages where the spouse, in this case often the man, departs to stay with his girl friend. After a while he returns and promises to stay at home, which he does for a variable interval only to return to the girl friend. The unhappy wife asks how often she has to take him back? Once again the decision must be hers but, in practice, a man who behaves in this way is showing marked ambivalent behaviour. Often he wants the security of his home, the presence of his children, and the desire not to hurt his wife, but his emotional and sexual commitment is with his girl friend. In practice the upheaval of such recurrent departures is immense. The wife and children suffer repeatedly the process of loss then, just as they are settling down to a new routine, the husband returns. The situation becomes intolerable and it seems justified that a wife who is still prepared to consider taking her husband back (and such an attitude needs clarification: Why does she want him back?) should insist that he seeks help, only accepting him back when he has made progress with his emotional ambivalence. Often the man seeks help and still cannot decide where he wants to stay, in which case the wife can be justified in refusing further readmissions to the matrimonial home.

Children

Staying and departing for the sake of the children is the most cruel and difficult decision. There is no unequivocal evidence to point clearly to what should be done. It seems to me that there are two separate questions. The first is the viability of the marriage in its own right. Spouses have to decide whether their marriage is viable or not and whether anything can be done to improve it. Thus the first issue is the state of the marriage. It goes without saying that when children are present most parents will do their utmost to stay together for their own sake and for that of the children. But what happens when the marriage is not viable in the way described above? This is where no one can decide the complex issues except the couple themselves. If the marriage is not viable but there are young children who have, say, ten to fifteen years to go before reaching adulthood, should the parents stay for their sake? A previous generation with different social, moral and religious standards would have answered mostly in the positive: Yes, they should stay. Today contemporary couples do not necessarily give the same answer. The easy comment is to describe their decision as selfish, and in fact many people do call such parents selfish. Even those who have a religious belief that condemns divorce should remember not to make judgements against their neighbour. The pain and cost of marital breakdown is immense, without the addition of moral judgements which, in any case, do not belong to the sphere of professional advice.

But moral judgements apart, do we know whether children are damaged by marital breakdown? This is an exceedingly difficult question to answer. From an extensive literature which has investigated the cognitive and emotional problems of divorce, the work of Wallerstein & Kelley (1980) who followed up divorced children for up to five years, showed that a percentage remained hurt throughout the period of observation. Clearly divorce is far more traumatic to children than was once believed. Recent work (Mitchell, 1985) suggests that children want their parents to stay together, even if they are fighting.

But what if the couple do stay with the children? Here the outcome depends on whether the atmosphere is charged with hostility, argument and aggression which is detrimental, or whether the relationship of the parents is one of amicable indifference when it is less so.

Outcome of Therapy/Counselling

Therapy/counselling is normally undertaken with the aim of reaching a stable, contented relationship. But this is not always the outcome. On some occasions a spouse who is unhappy but trapped in the marriage seeks help. This may be a dependent wife or an anxious and insecure husband. In the course of therapy they gain in strength, confidence and security. After several months or even years they feel they can leave their spouse. In other words, therapy/counselling which starts as a process of reconciliation can end in a final separation. This is something that should be taken into consideration when clients are received for help. When clinical experience suggests that such an outcome is possible and likely, then it is appropriate to warn the person of such a possibility right at the beginning. It is even more important to warn the partner of such an outcome.

Conclusion

It can be seen that the task of the therapist/counsellor in the case where advice is asked about separation is to clarify. The decision must always be left to the individual but with the expert and informed help of the counsellor, whose task is not to influence the decision one way or another but to ensure that the facts are available so that the client is armed with the relevant insight.

References

Adelstein, A. and White, A., 1976, *Population Trends* No. 6, HMSO, London.

Ballard, R., 1959, *American Journal of Orthopsychiatry*, 29, 547.
Ballinger, C.B., 1975, *British Medical Journal*, III, 344.
Bancroft, J. et al., 1977, *Psychological Medicine*, 7, 289.
Bernard, J., 1966, *Journal of Marriage and the Family*, 31, 209.
Blood, R.O. and Wolfe, D.M., 1960, *Husbands and Wives, the Dynamics of Married Living*, Free Press, New York.
Bloom, B.L. et al., 1977, *Journal of Divorce*, 1, 7.
Bourne, S. and Lewis, E., 1984, *British Medical Journal*, 289, 147.
Bowlby, J., 1979, *The Making and Breaking of Affectionate Bonds*, Tavistock Publications, London.
Brannen, J. and Collard, J., 1982, *Marriage in Trouble: the process of seeking help*, Tavistock Publications, London and New York.
Breen, J., 1975, *The Birth of a First Child*, Tavistock Publication, London.
Briscoe, C.W., 1973, *Archives of General Psychiatry*, 29, 119.
Brown, A. and Kiernan, K. E., 1981, *Population Trends* No.25, HMSO, London.
Brown, G.W. and Harris, I., 1978, *Social Origins of Depression*, Tavistock Publications, London.

Chester, R., 1971, *British Journal of Sociology*, 22, 172.
Chester, R., 1972, *Postgraduate Medical Journal*, 48, 529.
Chester, R., 1972, *Journal of Biosocial Service*, 4, 443.
Christensen, H.T. and Rubinstein, B.B., 1956, *Marriage and Family Living*, 18, 114.
Christensen, H.T., 1973, *Eugenics Quarterly*, 10, 119.
Clulow, C.F., 1982, *To Have and To Hold*, Aberdeen University Press, Aberdeen.
Coleman, D.A., 1977, "Assortative Mating in Britain" in *Equalities and Inequalities in Family Life*, ed. R. Chester and J. Peel, Academic Press, London.

Coleman, K.H., 1980, *Journal of Psychology*, 105, 197.

Coombs, L.C. and Zumeta, Z., 1970, *Social Problems*, 18, 92.

Cox, J.L. et al., 1982, *British Journal of Psychiatry*, 140, 111.

Crow, M.J., 1973, *Journal of Psychosomatic Research*, 17, 309.

Crow, M.J., 1978, *Psychological Medicine*, 8, 623.

Curtis, J.L., 1955, *U.S. Armed Forces Medical Journal*, 6, 937.

Dalton, K., 1968, *Depression after Childbirth*, Oxford University Press, Oxford.

DHSS, 1976, *Prevention and Health: Everybody's Business*, HMSO, London.

Dicks, H.V., 1967, *Marital Tensions*, Routledge and Kegan Paul, London.

Dominian, J., 1968, *Marital Breakdown*, Penguin, London.

Dominian, J., 1980, *Marital Pathology*, Darton, Longman and Todd, London.

Dominian, J., 1981, *Marriage, Faith and Love*, Darton, Longman and Todd (and Fount Paperbacks, 1984), London.

Dominian, J., 1984, *Make or Break*, S.P.C.K., London.

Edward, G. and Gross, M.M., 1976, *British Medical Journal*, 1, 1058.

Erikson, E.H., 1968, *Identity*, Faber and Faber, London.

Eysenck, H.J., 1967, *The Biological Basis of Personality*, C.C. Thomas, Springfield, Illinois.

Eysenck, H.J., 1978, *Sex and Personality*, Abacus, London.

Fairbairn, W.R.D., 1967, *An Object Relations Theory of the Personality*, Basic Books, New York.

Fisher, G., 1973, *The Female Orgasm*, Basic Books, New York.

Frommer, E.A. and O'Shea, G., 1973, *British Journal of Psychiatry*, 123, 149.

Frommer, E.A. and O'Shea, G., 1973, *British Journal of Psychiatry*, 123, 157.

Fullberg, J., 1972, in *Psychosomatic Medicine in Obstetrics and Gynaecology*, Kerger, Basle.

Furstenberg, F.F., 1976, *Journal of Social Issues*, 32, 67.

Gayford, J., 1975, *British Medical Journal*, 1, 194.

Gelles, R., 1972, *The Violent Home: Sage Library of Social Research 13*, Sage Publications.

Gibson, C., 1974, *British Journal of Sociology*, 25, 79.

Glick, P.C. and Norton, A.J., 1971, *Journal of Marriage and the Family*, 33, 307.

Goldstein, M.K., 1971, *Behavior Rate Change in Marriage: Training Wives to Moderate their Husbands' Behavior*. Ph.D. Dissertation, Cornell University, New York.

Gottman, J. et al., 1976, *A Couple's Guide to Communication*, Research Press, Illinois.

Granville-Grossman, K.L., 1971, in *Recent Advances in Clinical Psychiatry*, J.A. Churchill, London.

Guerney, B.G., Jr., 1977, *Relationship Enhancement*, Jossey-Bass, San Francisco.

Hamilton, J.A., 1962, *Post Partum Psychiatric Problems*, Mosby, St Louis.

Hare, E.H. and Shaw, G.K., 1965, *British Journal of Psychiatry*, III, 461.

Haskey, J., 1980, *Population Trends No.22*, 19, HMSO, London.

Haskey, J., 1982, *Population Trends No.27*, HMSO, London.

Haskey, J., 1983, *Population Trends No.31*, HMSO, London.

Haskey, J., 1983, *Population Trends No.32*, HMSO, London.

Hobbs, D.F. and Cole, S.P., 1976, *Journal of Marriage and the Family*, 38, 723.

Homans, G.C., 1950, *On Human Group*, Harcourt Brace, New York.

Horney, K., 1969, in J.A.C. Brown, *Freud and the Post Freudians*, Penguin, London.

Ineichen, B., 1977, "Youthful Marriage: The Vortex of Disadvantage" in *Equalities and Inequalities in Family Life*, ed. R. Chester and J. Peel, Academic Press, London.

Isaacs, S., 1972, *British Medical Journal*, 3, 224.

Jacobson, P.H., 1950, *American Sociological Review*, 15, 235.

Jellinek, E.K., 1952, *Quarterly Journal Studies of Alcohol*, 13, 673.

Kaplan, H.S., 1974, *The New Sex Therapy*, Brummer Mazel, New York.

Kersch, N., 1965, *British Medical Journal*, 2, 1265.

Kiernan, K.E., 1983, *Occasional Paper, 31*, OPCS, London.

Kinsey, A.G. et al., 1948, *Sexual Behavior in the Human Male*, Saunders, Philadelphia.

Kinsey, A.G. et al., 1953, *Sexual Behavior in the Human Female*, Saunders, Philadelphia.

Klein, M., 1957, *Envy and Gratitude*, Tavistock Publication, London.

Klein, M., 1959, *Our Adult World and Its Roots in Infancy*, Tavistock Publications, London.

Klein, M., 1965, *Contributions to Psychoanalysis 1921-1945*, Hogarth Press, London.

Kreitman, N., 1964, *British Journal of Psychiatry*, 110, 159.

Kreitman, N., 1970, *British Journal of Psychiatry*, 117, 33.

Kumar, R. and Robson, K., 1978, in *Mental Illness in Pregnancy and the Puerperium*, ed. M. Sandler, Oxford Medical Publications, Oxford.

Lacousiere, R.B., 1972, *Psychiatric Quarterly*, 46, 109.

Leete, R. and Anthony, S., 1979, *Population Trends* No.16, HMSO, London.

Le Masters, E.E., 1957, *Marriage and Family Living*, 19, 352.

Levinger, G., 1966, *American Journal of Orthopsychiatry*, 36, 804.

Liberman, R.P., 1970, *American Journal of Orthopsychiatry*, 40, 106.

Liberman, R.P. et al., 1976, *Journal of Marriage and Family Counselling*, 2, 383.

Lidz, J., 1976, *The Person – His and Her Development Throughout the Life Cycle*, Basic Books, New York.

McGregor, O.R. et al., 1970, *Separated Spouses*, Duckworth, London.

Mansfield, P., 1982, *National Marriage Guidance Council*, Rugby, NMGC.

Mansfield, P., 1986, *Just Married*, (in press).

Masters, W. and Johnson, V.E., 1970, *Human Sexual Inadequacy*, Churchill, London.

Mickelson, D.J. and Stevic, R.R., 1971, *Journal of Consulting Psychology*, 18, 314.

Mitchell, A.K., 1981, *Someone To Turn To*, Aberdeen University Press, Aberdeen.

Mitchell, A.K., 1985, *Children in the Middle: living through divorce*, Tavistock Publications, London.

Mitchell, A.R.K., 1978, *Violence in the Family*, Wayland, Hove.

Monahan, T.P., 1960, *Eugenics Quarterly*, 7, 140.

Murphy, M., 1984, *Journal of Biosocial Science*, 16, 487.

Murray, R.M., 1975, *Journal of Alcoholism*, 10, 23.

Oakley, A., 1979, *Being a Mother*, Martin Robertson, London.

Oakley, A., 1980, *Women Confined*, Martin Robertson, London.

O'Brien, J., 1971, *Journal of Marriage and the Family*, 33, 4, 692.

O'Leary, R.D. and Turkewitz, H., 1978, "Marital Therapy from a

Behavioral . . .", in Paolini, T.J. and McGrady, B.S. (eds), *Marriage and Marital Therapy: Psychoanalytic, Behavioral and Systems Theory Perspective*, Brummer Mazel, New York.

OPCS, 1980, *Marriage and Divorce Statistics*, Series FM2, HMSO, London.

Oppenheimer, E.H., 1984, *Marriage and Health*, Marriage Research Centre, London.

Oxford, J. and Guthrie, S., 1976, "Alcoholic Dependence", in Edwards, G., Russel, M.A.H., Hawks, D. and MacCafferty, M. (eds).

Ovenstone, I.M.K., 1973, *British Journal of Psychiatry*, 122, 35.

Ovenstone, I.M.K., 1973, *British Journal of Psychiatry*, 122, 711.

Paolini, T.J. and McGrady, B.S., 1977, *The Alcoholic Marriage: Alternative Perspective*, Greene and Stralton, New York.

Paton, A. et al., 1984, *ABC of Alcohol – Articles from the BMJ*, British Medical Journal, London.

Paykel, E.S. et al., 1969, *Archives of General Psychiatry*, 21, 753.

Pierce, R.M., 1963, *Sociological Review*, 11, 215.

Pitt, B., 1968, *British Journal of Psychiatry*, 114, 1325.

Population Trends, 1985, No.39, Office of Population Censuses and Surveys, HMSO, London.

Protheroe, C., 1969, *British Journal of Psychiatry*, 128, 379.

Robins, A.A., 1962, *Psychiatric Quarterly*, 36, 129.

Rollings, B.C. and Cannon, K.L. 1974, *Journal of Marriage and the Family*, 36, 271.

Rowntree, G., 1964, *Population Studies*, 18, 147.

Shepherd, M., 1961, *Journal of Marital Science*, 107, 687.

Shepherd, M. et al., 1966, *Psychiatric Illness in General Practice*, Oxford University Press, Oxford.

Sholevar, G.P. (ed.), 1981, *The Handbook of Marriage and Marital Therapy*, MTP Press, New York.

Skegg, D.C. et al., 1977, *British Medical Journal*, 1, 1561.

Skinner, B.F., 1953, *Science and Human Behavior*, Macmillan, New York.

Smith, S., 1973, *British Medical Journal*, 4, 385.

Smith, S., 1974, *British Journal of Psychiatry*, 125, 568.

Smith, S. and Hanson, R., 1974, *British Medical Journal*, 3, 666.

Smith, S. and Hanson, R., 1975, *British Journal of Psychiatry*, 127, 513.

Snaith, R.P., 1983, *British Journal of Hospital Medicine*, 29 (5), 450.

Sneddon, J. and Kerry, R.J., 1980, *British Journal of Psychiatry*, 132, 164.

Social Trends, 1976, No.7, HMSO, London.

Social Trends, 1985, No.15, HMSO, London.

Stein, G., 1982, in *Motherhood and Mental Illness*, ed. Brockington, I.F. and Kumar, R., Academic Press, London.

Steinglass, P. et al., 1971, *Archives of General Psychiatry*, 24, 401.

Steinmetz, S., 1980, *Annals of New York Academy of Science*, 347, 251.

Stuart, R.B., 1969, *Journal of Consultative and Clinical Psychology*, 33, 675.

Tharp, R.G., 1963, *Psychological Bulletin*, 60, 97.

Thibaut, J. and Kelley, H.H., 1959, *The Social Psychology of Groups*, Wiley, New York.

Thornes, B. and Collard, J., 1979, *Who Divorces?*, Routledge and Kegan Paul, London.

Todd, E.D.M., 1964, *Lancet*, II, 1264.

Truaz, C.V. and Carkhuff, R.R., 1967, *Toward Effective Counselling and Psychotherapy Training and Practice*, Aldine, Chicago.

Udenberg, N., 1974, *Journal of Psychosomatic Research*, 18, 33.

Walker, C., 1977, in *Equalities and Inequalities in Family Life*, Academic Press, London.

Walker, K.E., 1969, *Family Economics Review*, 5, 6.

Wallerstein, J.S. and Kelley, J.B., 1980, *Surviving the Breakdown*, Grant McIntyre.

Watson, J.P. et al., 1984, *British Journal of Psychiatry*, 144, 453.

Watzlawick, P., Brown, J. and Jackson, D., 1967, *Pragmatics of Human Communication*, W.W. Norton, New York.

Weiss, R.L. et al., 1973, in L.A. Hamenlynk, L.C. Handy and E.J. Mayse (eds), *Behavior Change: Methodology, Concepts and Practice*, Research Press, Illinois.

Weissman, M.M. and Klerman, G.L., 1977, *Archives of General Psychiatry*, 34, 98.

Whallen, T., 1953, *Quarterly Journal of Studies on Alcohol*, 14, 632.

Winnicott, D.W., 1965, *The Family and Individual Development*, Tavistock Publication, London.

Wrate, R.M. et al., 1985, *British Journal of Psychiatry*, 146, 622.

Index

Fount Paperbacks

Fount is one of the leading paperback publishers of religious books and below are some of its recent titles.

- [ ] THE WAY OF ST FRANCIS Murray Bodo £2.50
- [ ] GATEWAY TO HOPE Maria Boulding £1.95
- [ ] LET PEACE DISTURB YOU Michael Buckley £1.95
- [ ] DEAR GOD, MOST OF THE TIME YOU'RE QUITE NICE Maggie Durran £1.95
- [ ] CHRISTIAN ENGLAND VOL 3 David L Edwards £4.95
- [ ] A DAZZLING DARKNESS Patrick Grant £3.95
- [ ] PRAYER AND THE PURSUIT OF HAPPINESS Richard Harries £1.95
- [ ] THE WAY OF THE CROSS Richard Holloway £1.95
- [ ] THE WOUNDED STAG William Johnston £2.50
- [ ] YES, LORD I BELIEVE Edmund Jones £1.75
- [ ] THE WORDS OF MARTIN LUTHER KING Coretta Scott King (Ed) £1.75
- [ ] BOXEN C S Lewis £4.95
- [ ] THE CASE AGAINST GOD Gerald Priestland £2.75
- [ ] A MARTYR FOR THE TRUTH Grazyna Sikorska £1.95
- [ ] PRAYERS IN LARGE PRINT Rita Snowden £2.50
- [ ] AN IMPOSSIBLE GOD Frank Topping £1.95
- [ ] WATER INTO WINE Stephen Verney £2.50

All Fount paperbacks are available at your bookshop or newsagent, or they can be ordered by post from Fount Paperbacks, Cash Sales Department, G.P.O. Box 29, Douglas, Isle of Man, British Isles. Please send purchase price, plus 15p per book, maximum postage £3. Customers outside the U.K. send purchase price, plus 15p per book. Cheque, postal or money order. No currency.

NAME (Block letters) _____

ADDRESS _____

_____

While every effort is made to keep prices low, it is sometimes necessary to increase them at short notice. Fount Paperbacks reserve the right to show new retail prices on covers which may differ from those previously advertised in the text or elsewhere.